Vimy Ridge

Kenneth Macksey

Pan/Ballantine

Editor-in-Chief: Barrie Pitt
Editor: David Mason
Art Director: Sarah Kingham
Picture Editor: Robert Hunt
Consultant Art Editor: Denis Piper
Designer: David A Evans
Illustration: John Batchelor
Photographic Research: Jonathan Moore
Cartographer: Michael Hine

Photographs for this book were especially selected from the following archives: from left to right pages 4–5 Imperial War Museum, London; 7 Canadian National Archives; 8–9 IWM; 10 Suddeutscher Verlag, Munich; 11 US National Archives; 14–14 IWM; 14 Canadian Archives; 17–19 US Archives; 20 Bibliothek Nationale, Paris; 23 US Archives; 26–27 Canadian Archives; 28–29 IWM; 31 US Archives; 32–33 IWM; 34–35 Suddeutscher; 35–41 IWM; 42–43 Canadian Archives; 45 Suddeutscher; 49–50 US Archives; 51 Canadian Archives; 52–53 US Archives; 54–61 IWM; 61 Suddeutscher; 62 US Archives; 62–68 IWM; 68–73 Canadian Archives; 74–75 IWM; 76–77 US Archives; 78 IWM; 80–81 Canadian Archives; 84–85 IWM; 88–91 Canadian Archives; 92–93 IWM; 94–97 Canadian Archives; 96–98 IWM; 99 Canadian Archives; 100–101 IWM; 103–105 US Archives; 109 IWM; 111 US Archives; 111-120 IWM; 125 US Archives; 127 Bundesarchiv, Koblenz; 131–135 IWM; 136 Canadian Archives; 139 US Archives; 140 Suddeutscher; 140 IWM; 144 Suddeutscher; 145 US Archives; 146 Suddeutscher; 146 US Archives; 149 Suddeutscher; 152 IWM; 154–155 US Archives; 156–157 Canadian Archives; 157 US Archives; 158–159 IWM; Front cover, Imperial War Museum; Back cover, Canadian National Archives

ISBN 0 330 23839 6

First published in the United States 1972
This Pan/Ballantine edition published 1973 by
Pan Books Ltd, 33 Tothill Street, London SW1

Printed in Great Britain by
Butler and Tanner Ltd, Frome and London

Contents

8 The proving ground
16 Dawn of an obsession
30 The coming of the British
42 The knife edge
54 The Hindenburg Line
64 The guns take charge
80 Easter Monday
102 Towards Cambrai
112 Study in surprises
126 The breaking strain
138 Pendulum
148 The final sally

The bastion

Introduction by Barrie Pitt

In 1914 the Schlieffen Plan flung the German armies across Belgium and the north-eastern provinces of France in a gigantic wheel, pivoted on the Vosges Mountains; it was intended to sweep westwards of Paris, then eastwards to entrap the French armies and crush them against their own fortifications and the Swiss border. The plan failed because of the impossibility of feeding, supplying and reinforcing the armies on the rim of the wheel across the enormous expanse of the battleground they covered – combined with weaknesses of mind and nerve in the German High Command. As a result, the radius of the wheel contracted, the outer armies swung in east of Paris and exposed themselves to flank attack from the French garrison in the capital, while the remainder of the French armies, instead of being trapped, were merely pressed back along their own lines of communication.

Thus when the exhausted German troops reached the Marne, sweltering in the August heat, they were held as though in the bottom of a sack by the re-formed and recuperating Allied line. Every attempt they made to thrust across the top of the sack and renew their sweep westwards was countered by extensions of the Allied line to the north until it stretched up through Amiens, across the Belgian frontier and the Flanders plain, and ended on the sea between Nieuport and Ostend. In the meantime, pressure on the bottom of the sack forced the central German armies to recoil along their own tracks – and now the situation developed as before, but in reverse; as the German lines of communication shortened, the French stretched. Eventually, positions of balance were reached where neither of the forces facing each other could move forward without additional strength – and each unit feverishly dug defensive positions to hold until reinforcements should come up in sufficient numbers to enable them to break through the enemy line opposite.

Thus the trench line formed and the

stalemate which was to last for four long years began.

From the Belgian coast near Nieuport the lines and the strips of war-wasted ground between and behind them lay smeared across the land like the trail of a gigantic snail. It left the sand-dunes of the coast in a fifteen-mile southerly curve, then bulged out eastward and back again like the outline of a chancre around the murdered landscape of the Ypres Salient; then, just south of Ypres, the flat plain is broken for the first time. As Major Macksey says when setting the scene for this lucid and evocative account: 'Standing firm in the centre of the Western front and coveted with predatory zeal by both sides alike, the fields around Arras and, in particular, the Heights of Vimy, were to serve as a proving ground for the slow evolution of new techniques.'

The Germans got there first – it would seem that in those opening days they had a better eye for ground than the Allies – and as a result commanded the field of battle in a semi-circle to the west for a radius of ten miles. But such a position of supremacy exacts its own price, for the Allies in turn made it a focal point for their efforts and, as months passed, more and more Frenchmen and Englishmen, and more and more of the Allied munitions of war, were to be devoted to wresting the ridge from its holders.

Eventually, Vimy Ridge was to be the scene of the first spectacular triumph of the young Canadian Army, and as such its name and the story of its capture is perhaps the main foundation stone of Canada's military tradition – a tradition superbly upheld in many theatres of war between 1939 and 1945. Canadian troops remained on the heights until October 1918, when they moved forward to take part in the pursuit of the German Army back over the Rhine.

Theirs was undoubtedly the most glorious role in the saga of Vimy Ridge, but French valour, British determination and German stubborness all played their part in that saga.

The proving ground

When in 1905 General von Schlieffen completed his scheme for an all-enveloping wheel by the German army through the Low Countries into Northern France, so vast was the scope of his concept that almost the entire span of the northern French provinces would have been engulfed. It was intended that a swelling concourse of marching armies should expand outwards from the German frontier to Antwerp, through the important Belgian industrial complex and thence into France – to Lille and Lens with their coalfields. The preponderant German right flank formation, their First Army, would scythe far to the west within sight of the English Channel, crossing the River Somme near its estuary at the extremity of an arc to sweep round the western environs of Paris. In one swoop the communication centres of France – rail, road and waterway junctions such as Douai, Arras and Amiens – would fall into German hands along with the ports giving access to the British should they choose to intervene. The brain of the country would be paralysed and – of less political value, though of important military effect – a base, from which attacks against the German wheel could be launched, would be eliminated.

German infantry cut the first trenches in 1914

General Schlieffen

General Moltke

But while grandiose military plans are compelling to facile imaginations – and quite appalling in peacetime when their intent is calculated for untrammelled aggression – the Schlieffen plan demanded too much of its executants. Not even Germany, with an economy bent deliberately towards war making, was able to raise the manpower and industrial output that could satisfy Schlieffen's requirements. Moreover, for any chance of success, the plan demanded the vital guidance of a daring strategist such as Schlieffen was. But Schlieffen's successor of 1906, General Helmuth von Moltke, was anything but that. Yet is was to be Moltke's destiny to preside not only over the watering down of the original plan but also to put it into operation in 1914. More and more he had come to fear the threat from Russia in the east and, in response, took forces from the west to meet it. Inexorably the right flank wheel had to be diluted and constricted until it became the ghost of what Schlieffen had originally envisaged. By August 1914 the German wheel would have contracted on its centre, the extreme right flank of First Army turning short of Douai, missing Arras and Amiens, to aim direct through Mons upon Paris. Only a cavalry screen would project a tenuous German presence among these places, leaving intact a base for an Anglo-French counter offensive on the western flank.

Vimy Ridge, a stark promontory rising 400 feet above the western edge of the wide Plain of Douai, is a natural buttress jutting from out of the hilly interior of the Pas de Calais. It was a fine place from which to observe the angry flush of war crossing the plain as Anglo-French armies withdrew upon Paris in August 1914. Each day the growl of battle became louder and each night the glow from burning towns and homesteads crept closer. Soon the day came when skirmishing broke out nearby between scantily equipped and poorly trained French

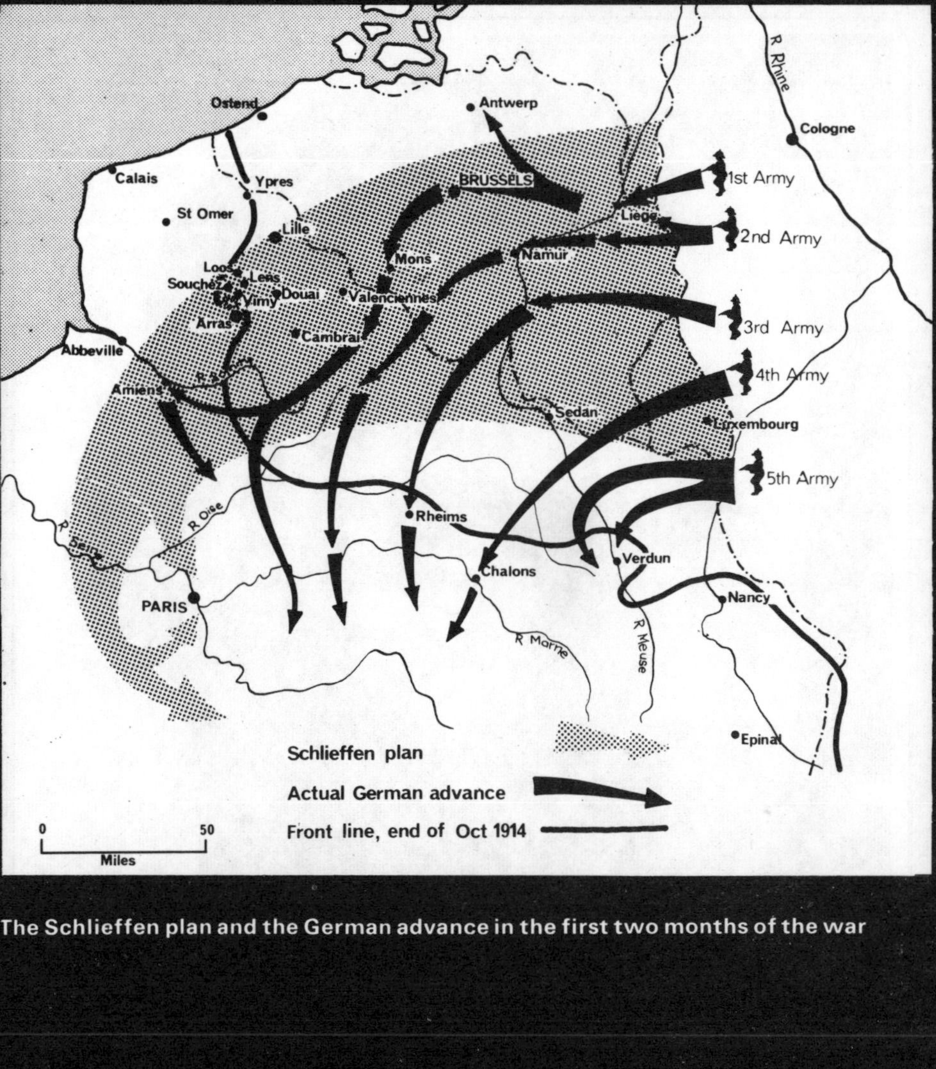

The Schlieffen plan and the German advance in the first two months of the war

territorial infantry and the highly professional German cavalry patrols that probed and foraged with scant restraint. For three days, from 6th to 9th September, Arras lay under occupation of a regiment of horse, and all was in flux until French cavalry arrived from the south to drive them away. Vimy Ridge once more came into French hands as Allied fortunes blossomed at the Battle of the Marne and the German strategic withdrawal began. But now began a new phase in a war so unlike any that had been seen before – a war which was to grind this narrow corner of Europe, with Arras and Vimy Ridge at its centre, to dust. The celebrated 'Race to the Sea' was in progress as the opposing armies attempted successively to outflank each other in a northerly direction, leaving in their train a necklace of continuous and invulnerable trenches held fast by barbed wire and a thin but deadly array of artillery and machine-gun positions.

As fast as men could march and railways could transfer the vast accoutrements of bombardment and assault from one place to the next, the trench lines were extended and then solidified. On 21st September it was decided by the German High Command to transfer their Sixth Army, under Crown Prince Rupprecht, from the left flank, in the Vosges Mountains, and concentrate it in the Plain of Douai, west of Cambrai, there to spearhead a pale reactivation of the original Schlieffen Plan by a westward drive through Arras, towards the English Channel, prior to swinging south across the Somme between Amiens and Abbeville. Yet concurrently the French Tenth Army, newly formed under General de Maud'huy, was also beginning its deployment in the vicinity of Arras with its X Corps aligned close to the east of the city and upon the slopes of Vimy Ridge, and its XXI Corps stretched further north guarding the approaches to the ridge overlooking Lens.

General Kronprinz Rupprecht

Against these two corps would fall the full weight of Rupprecht's three infantry corps plus the German Cavalry Corps, under General von der Marwitz. But each successive outflanking move by the horsemen was to be bloodily parried by French infantry. The sort of combat which was to dominate the First World War on the Western Front was being invented on the slopes of Vimy Ridge.

Denied the hoped-for breakthrough past Arras and across Vimy Ridge to the coast, the Germans paused to gain further strength, replacing cavalry with infantry and guns. Meanwhile, de Maud'huy was preparing his own offensive with the intention of driving the Germans eastwards and clearing the Plain, thus liberating the captured industrial zone around Lille. But the Germans were ready first, pushing hard against Arras on 2nd October, pummelling the French with a storm of field-artillery fire and thrusting them back by the combined assault of the three infantry corps which lapped the outskirts of Arras, rolled to the foot of Vimy Ridge, climbed its steep slope, thence to plunge confidently southwest, to drive past Souchez, Carency and Mont St Eloy, before debouching upon the western city limits in an attempt to complete an encirclement. For close on a week German Sixth and French Tenth Armies grappled in repeated charge and countercharge. Gun fought gun while solid masses of men and horses advanced in hordes to the slaughter. On 9th October exhaustion finally ended the struggle. The French had held firm and the Germans were forced to desist and shift their attention yet further northwards. There, too, successive thrusts would terminate at Ypres in hideous stalemate in this final attempt at turning the Allied line.

By mid-November the entire Western Front was deadlocked by the encroaching web of trenches. The original German attempt at unmitigated conquest had failed in parallel with French hopes for a march on Berlin.

Above: German artillery helps seal the front. *Below:* Arras Cathedral, first target for the German guns

In the process, however, rather more than a campaign had collapsed and been cheated of its forecast decisive conclusion. A military myth enshrined as doctrine had been destroyed–the demolition of a belief that attacking masses, their morale enhanced by an unquenchable will to conquer, could overcome the sheer volume and killing power of modern arms. Nobody in authority before the war had calculated with mathematical certainty that the density of fire projected by quick-firing artillery, machine-guns and rifles would devastate the energy produced by mass as multiplied by velocity. Mere men, hopelessly baffled, now took cover behind barricades or went below ground, appearing in the open only at night or to the accompaniment of a vast outlay of artillery fire whose object was to destroy, or at least numb, the enemy as an essential prelude to the traditional infantry assault. By trial and error this doleful practice was evolved by all seasoned combatants in 1914 and, in the succeeding years, developed to an art. War reverted to a system whereby a few clever men (they could even be of low physical calibre) operating machines of mass destruction could overcome the bravest of fully trained infantry. That being so the hopelessly vulnerable cavalry came to count for naught. And so infantry, the cheapest of all fighting elements, was doomed to impotence as its best men fell and those lesser trained took their place. Gradually, both sides would become aware that only machines could match machines and that victory would be the prize for technical advancement. Standing firm in the centre of the Western Front and coveted with predatory zeal by both contestants alike, the fields around Arras and, in particular, the Heights of Vimy, were to serve as proving grounds for the slow evolution of new techniques.

Dawn of an obsession

Vimy Ridge is composed of a chalk foundation overlain by heavy clay which, once soaked by water and churned by man, beast and wagon, converts into glutinous mud. The ridge is an outpost, shorn by a steep narrow valley from rolling hills which stretch the breadth of the Pas de Calais. In 1914 these hills shielded the Channel ports that were so vitally important to the British, if they were not to see a hostile German army encamped upon the cliffs above Boulogne and Calais. From the verge of this promontory, finger-shaped ridges reach towards the Plain of Douai, ridges of which the Heights of Vimy are a part, isolated in extension, but multiplied further eastwards where the nature of the topography changes. There, slopes falling steeply on either side of the principal ridges give way to smoother and easier gradients. The heights of Vimy Ridge themselves are sharp and abrupt on the promontory's north-eastern face, but the approaches from the south are rounder and gentler, giving no hint, as the crest is approached, of the coming plunge from above to the villages of Givenchy and Vimy below. Yet turning still further south from Vimy the folds become smoother, diminishing in undulations until the River Scarpe is reached, some three miles east of Arras at the village of Fampoux. On the other side of the river the definition of a ridge is almost entirely extinguished, though its vague shape can still be detected in knolls and dips that are the foothills of higher ground which overlook Arras from a distance of three miles or more.

Though the terrain changes shape at the cornerstone by Vimy village, the countryside's general aspect remains constant. Rolling farmland covers wide expanses where woods are small, few and far between. Numerous little red-bricked villages lie almost hidden below the crest lines, each village centred upon its church spire. The crests command the spires as each spire dominates its village – vital features in war when the possession of key observation posts becomes an obsession.

Rapidly this peaceful land became pockmarked by the instruments and excreta of combat. Immediately the natural observation posts on high ground and in church spires became the targets for guns whose controlling officers constructed strongpoints on the highest features. Then, as guns were dug deeper into pits, to avoid their opponents' wrath, the infantry, seeking safety from the guns and from

General Falkenhayn

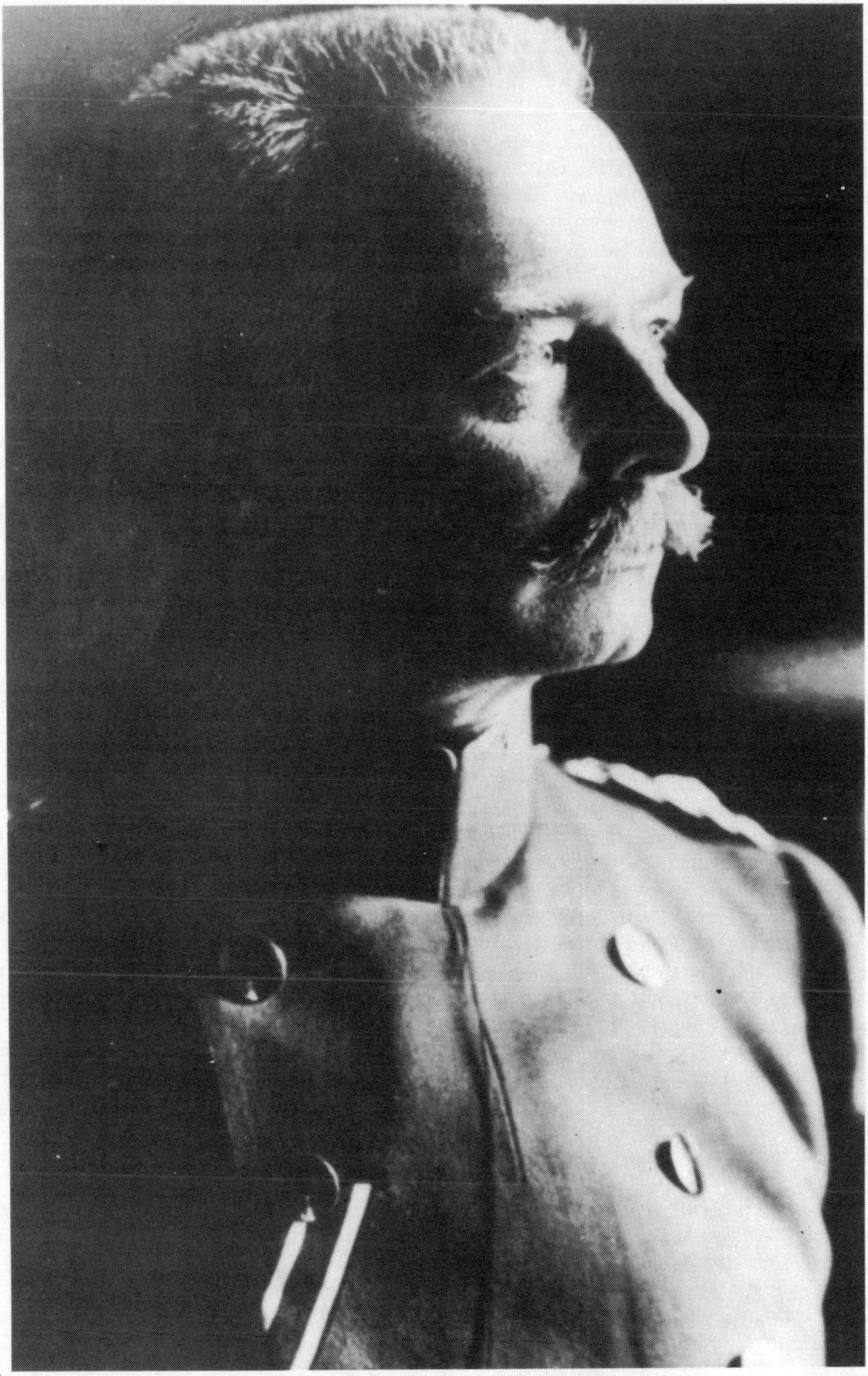

each other, linked their village strongpoints to the original shallow scrapes they had first dug in battle. A tracery of earthworks littered the landscape as a plague of shells began to dot and then carpet the fields, gradually erasing the farm buildings, then the villages and finally eating into Arras itself when German heavy artillery was unleashed upon the tallest buildings of the city on 21st October. Within a few hours the fabric of the old city was being destroyed. The people – those who had not already fled – had taken refuge in the cellars which previous generations had built for the purposes of commerce and for protection against hostile acts. Ever since it had become of importance as a route centre at the crossings of the Scarpe, Arras had attracted war. Siege, destruction and reconstruction were at the roots of its history but always its culture had survived. Now its vitality was to be taxed to the extreme in a state of partial siege.

The Germans had penetrated deeply either side of the city until they were brought to a halt in October. From the south, where the front line passed close to the village of Beaurains, from the east where it lay between the city boundary and the village of Tillois, and from the north where it intersected the road to Vimy near Roclincourt, light weapons could play directly upon the streets and squares. Moreover, the escape routes to the west, though kept firmly in French hands, were never free from the depredations of German guns whose fire could be brought accurately to bear on any point at the call of observers ensconced on the high ground – above all, from those who watched from the west and the north of Mont St Eloy, near Carency, and from certain vital pinnacles of Vimy Ridge – the heights known as Points 140 and 119.

Throughout the winter of 1914/1915, when both sides measured up to the task ahead and counted their deficiencies for a prolonged war, the Germans reduced their strength in the west in order to concentrate an offensive capability against Russia in the east. Their new Chief-of-Staff, General Erich von Falkenhayn, who had taken over from the failing Moltke after the latter's defeat at the Marne in September, turned east with reluctance. But he was impelled by the apparent need to prop up Germany's weakling yet principal ally, the Austro-Hungarian Empire, and urged on to his task by Generals Hindenburg and Ludendorff whose victories on the Eastern Front had shrouded them in the magical cloak of success. Germany's Kaiser Wilhelm yearned for success to justify a war of his own making and he tended to support most strongly of all those who gave it to him.

For the French High Command there was but one goal – the early liberation of French territory. Despite heavy losses and serious deficiencies in the materials of war, notably of heavy artillery and ammunition of all natures, they had won a tactical success in 1914. They looked only to enlarge upon it in 1915 until victory was won by the final ejection of the German army from those invaluable portions of occupied France. Then the defeat of their opponents would follow as by right. So, through a wearisome winter, while French armies under General Joffre persisted in a local and expensive offensive, a policy known as 'nibbling' ('I just keep nibbling', wrote Joffre as his army commanders were encouraged to make local attacks that sent tens of thousands to a wasteful and abortive death), plans for the valedictory offensive of 1915 were weighed and decided upon. A blow would be struck in the Champagne, but another far heavier in Artois at Vimy with the aim of moving north-eastwards, clearing the Ridge, lifting the siege of Arras and sweeping the Germans out of Douai (to the detriment of the railway system supplying their front) and the en-

General Joffre

French artillery, inadequate to its task

tire industrial zone to the north. Then the march on Berlin would be resumed.

Behind the planning of the French attack lay the enthusiasm of a man who was as dedicated to the offensive as he was to war itself – General Ferdinand Foch, who, as Commander of the Northern Group of armies, sold his scheme of attack to Joffre and imposed its details upon General d'Urbal whose Tenth Army was to execute it. The French attack was to be on a broad front. On the left, in the north, an eastward thrust by two divisions was to clear the long Lorette Spur until Souchez and Vimy Ridge beyond were overlooked from the west. In the centre an initial lunge by four divisions between Carency and Roclincourt was to carry the Ridge as the essential preliminary to exploitation by two reserve infantry and six cavalry divisions. On the right, in the south, an outward surge by infantry was to extend the zone of penetration over the ridge in the vicinity of the Point du Jour and free the suburbs of Arras along the north bank of the Scarpe. The main effort was to be aimed at the seizing of the ridge, a supremely strong position revealed in extensive photographs (gleaned by the new technique of aerial photography) as consisting of quadruple or sextuple lines of trenches at places such as the Lorette Spur, covering Ablain, the Labyrinth near Neuville St Vaast and the Point du Jour. If the Germans could be cleared from the Ridge their artillery and reserve positions would be exposed to French artillery installed on the high ground above the Douai Plain. French artillery, 780 field and 293 medium guns supplied by 690,000 rounds of ammunition, was to be the key to the assault, its technique a bombardment of selected German strongpoints (using but a fraction of the shells available) and then a massive barrage aimed along the front as the French infantry rose in a body, hoping to drive forward as much as 5,000 yards to their final objectives. It was assumed the leading divisions could accomplish this on their own; the reserve divisions were kept seven miles in rear, timed to march to the line only when initial success was so assured that the most profitable line of exploitation was recognisable. Outline planning was begun in February, intensified in March and the start set for 1st May. Later it was to be postponed to the 9th to allow more time for preparation – a trait which was to become a common deficiency in French battle procedures.

North of the La Bassée Canal, on the northern fringe of the French offensive, the British, too, were to play their part, taking over additional stretches of the line from the French to release extra divisions for the offensive and putting in their own attack in the direction of Aubers Ridge. The British had won a great reputation in 1914 as exponents of the defensive, but their prowess in attack had only recently been revealed in March at the Battle of Neuve Chapelle. Their resources, as yet, were so slight as to be incapable of a sustained effort, but the British army grew steadily in size, experience and stature and it had been joined already by sizeable contingents from its Dominions – an Indian corps of two divisions and the first division of Canadian troops (who underwent their battle innoculation at Ypres in April, playing a staunch part in stopping the surprise German gas attack). The preponderant part of the armies of the British Empire were being drawn to France's side on the Western Front despite diversions in Africa, Mesopotamia and Gallipoli though, as yet, their contribution was slim by comparison with that of the French.

The Germans were also compara-

French infantry, full of fire

tively weak in France, after diverting so many men to Hindenburg and Ludendorff for a major offensive against the Russians in Galicia. Rupprecht's Sixth Army still held the front opposite Arras but was heavily outnumbered, possessed as it was of just three divisions to secure this part of the line. Moreover 5th Bavarian Reserve Division, garrisoning Vimy Ridge, was two regiments under strength and had none for immediate backing. Even the army reserve, a mere two divisions, was stationed in Belgium at least two days march from the front and subject to GHQ control and delay. The front line troops were well dug-in, securely wired but lacking depth in deployment. Field artillery had difficulty in supporting the front line positions because it had to be situated on the forward slopes, otherwise its flat trajectory fire could not be brought to bear. The howitzers, with their high trajectory, were better off sheltering at the bottom of the reverse slope, but they were dependent on receiving orders by tenuous telephone communications from their observers on the crest, and almost impotent once shell fire had cut the cables. These would be the perennial German problems in holding the forward slope of Vimy Ridge – these and the fear that, once pushed back to the lip of the crest, they would literally be poised on the edge of disaster unless they withdrew some thousands of yards further to the east. Far more serious in May, however, was Rupprecht's total misunderstanding of the immediate threat. Neither he, his staff, nor the men at the front interpreted the French preparations as pointers to an offensive.

On the morning of 9th May, as the preparatory bombardment came to its end, the intense pre-assault phase began, the gunfire rising to a crescendo between 0600 hours and 1000 hours when, to quote a witness, the British General Henry Wilson, '. . . the guns stopped and the whole long line of French infantry . . . rose up out of their trenches and went forward. The next moment the guns opened again with a barrage. A most wonderful sight. I watched the infantry take all the trenches within sight with few losses and then, at 1100 hours I came away.' Wilson had been watching the central assault and here, indeed, success was won, the prize of complete surprise.

Up on the Lorette spur, unfortunately, the 13th Division had become enmeshed in German trenches and uncut barbed wire entanglements (French gunners picked their own targets, often without reference to their infantry's needs) and, in falling behind the cover provided by their artillery barrage, had become victims to those machineguns which had escaped damage and whose crews had recovered their composure. The spur remained in German hands. Yet such was success in the centre, where XXXIII Corps under General Pétain carried all before them, that failure on the Lorette might have been acceptable. 70th Division made progress down the adjoining southerly spur of Ablain, outflanking Carency from the north, while 77th Division did the same along the adjacent spur to the south. This latter division achieved even more, however, by overrunning the entire German front line position in the first hour, gathering an immense haul of terrified prisoners and continuing their progress through undefended country to the crest of Vimy Ridge. From there they saw the Plain of Douai revealed in full dramatic panorama – with hardly a German in sight. These Frenchmen had covered 5,000 yards – a formidable feat even on an exercise, but quite remarkable in action. Inevitably they had taken heavy casualties and lost cohesion but now, while they struggled in exhaustion to reorganise, was the moment for the climactic breakthrough by the fresh reserve divisions. Yet at this crucial moment the nearest reserves

General Maud'huy

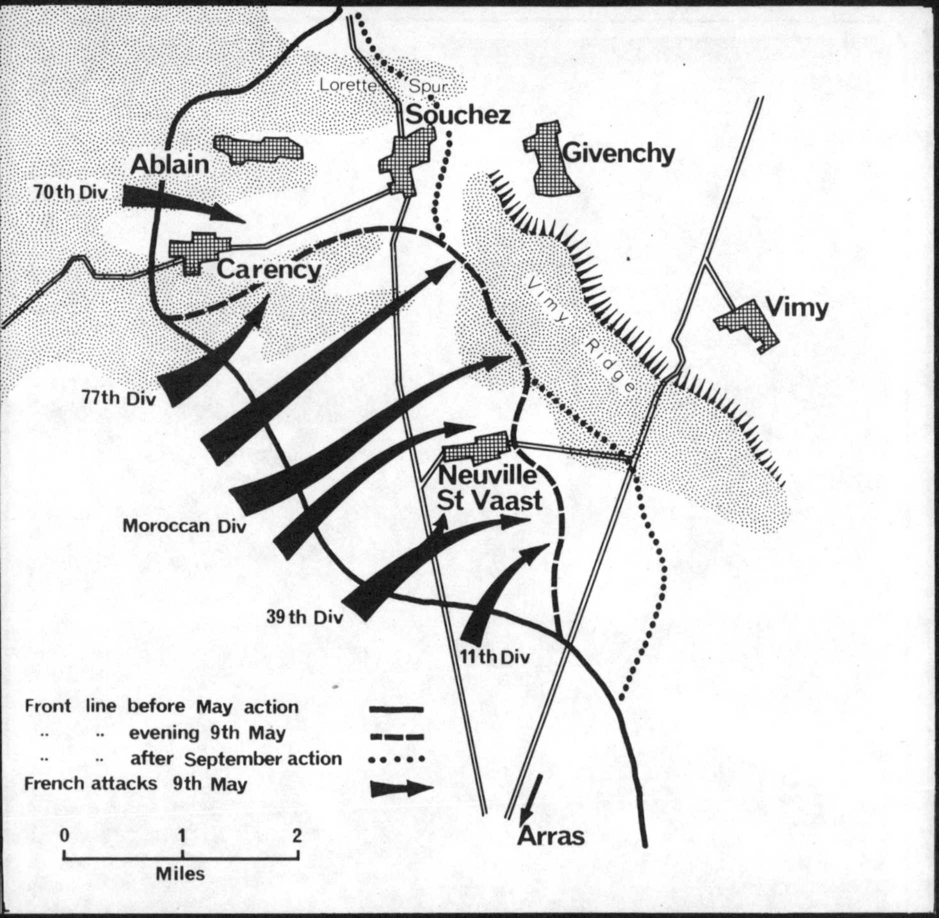

The French attacks of May and September 1915

were still seven miles distant and barely on the move. They would not arrive in the forefront of action, at the conquered Point 140, until 1830 hours but by then French freedom of movement was already impaired. For on the right of 77th Division the Légionnaires and Chasseurs of the superb, regular Moroccan Division, which had taken almost as much ground as the 77th, had become embroiled in a stiff fight for Neuville Vitasse where the Germans had held out. It then lost, too, many leaders, was worn down, and became incapable of further effort. So when at last the reserve division began to arrive in the dusk and found itself alone, not quite fresh and in unknown territory, it slowed down and became embroiled in the fight at Neuville from whence the ruptured German line began to coalesce. At this crucial moment, when the Germans were temporarily beaten, exploitation by the French would be limited to a mere few patrols creeping into the streets of Givenchy.

Reaction by the Germans was decisive. Rupprecht was delayed in moving his reserves by the need to obtain permission from GHQ. Only local counterattacks by scattered units, which had fortuitously avoided the initial holocaust, could be mounted. But, though the shoulders of the French salient were first contained, this would have been quite useless had the French merely pressed ahead instead of wasting what little strength their reserves possessed in fighting at the points of greatest resistance – namely the shoulders themselves. Lacking reinforcements, those units of the 77th Division which had reached the crest fell back. Joffre, Foch and d'Urbal might urge fresh divisions forward and bring cavalry close to the front, but the opportunity was lost and the ridge stayed firmly in German hands. For the next month or more, a whole series of local attacks were to be perpetrated, each more costly than its predecessor and gaining commensurately less ground, but none recreated the brazen chance of 9th May. With new divisions arriving and time to fit them into a reorganised line, Rupprecht could hold on – though only just. By 18th June, when Joffre called off the offensive, a mere strip of land, screening the top of Vimy Ridge and the Lorette Spur, remained in German hands. To the French the cost had come to something like 100,000 casualties, including those who had been utterly repulsed in attempting the breakout east of Arras. The Germans lost about 60,000 men.

War has an ugly knack of contriving emotional legends related to ideas or places, whether they be significant or trivial. Vimy Ridge was hardly trivial from the tactical aspect but its legend grew out of competing nationalistic urges until it got out of perspective. It became an obsession with both sides to gain and keep possession of the crest. Not only did they seek observation over the surrounding countryside but they came to regard possession of the Ridge as a symbol of victory and justification of blood already spilt. With characteristic thoroughness the Germans dug deep and honeycombed their wafer-thin slice of the Ridge with underground works, fearful that if they were budged a mere furlong backwards they would be utterly defeated. And the French got up steam for a renewed attempt to finally overcome by brute force what had baffled them before.

Throughout the summer Joffre's plans matured, although, in essence, they were remarkably similar to those which had already failed. Because so much of the Western Front line passed through tortuous country that was unsuitable for large scale operations or failed to point in the direction of a worthwhile strategic objective, his choice of battlefield once more fell automatically on Champagne and Artois, though priority was given to the former locality. Renewed assaults were to be launched in both areas in September. Again the British were to collaborate by taking over additional stretches of the line (this time a long stretch from the south of Arras to the valley of the Somme), in order to release more French troops for the assault, and they themselves were also to attack in the north, this time at Loos, on a grander scale than ever before.

The strategic objective in Artois remained fixed on the railway centre at Douai, and though French tactics were varied they were not drastically changed. Reserves would be positioned closer to the front to take quick advantage of ephemeral success, and the artillery would be instructed to bend to necessity and direct their fire specifically against those obstacles that constituted the infantry's chief perils – the wire and the machinegun posts. By now, the volume of fire which could be projected had vastly increased. Many more medium guns and greater stocks of ammunition became available so that, for this attack against Vimy Ridge, d'Urbal would have at his disposal 420 mediums on a twelve-mile front as opposed to 290 before. But everything would still depend on the *élan* of the infantry – and the infantry were at last beginning to show signs of disillusionment.

While French striking power had been only marginally increased, that of the Germans had been enormously strengthened by improved efficiency. However, a crippling shortage of manpower stretched Rupprecht's divisions to breaking point and yet again he was astonishingly unaware of the impending storm – largely because his reconnaissance aircraft found it almost impossible to cross the line in the face of superior Allied combat aircraft which chased the previously dominant Fokker single-seater fighters from the sky. As an aid to the land battle air power was as yet only an information agency and a superior observation post for artillery controllers. The most important improvement in German strength came from a deepening of the

The shattered battlefield

trench system at the expense of a considerable outlay in labour. Where a single row of front line trenches, backed by machinegun posts to its rear, had once been deemed sufficient, a double line now existed with strongpoints joined to the front by communication trenches, and with reserve battalions installed in the second line. In addition, a second main line on a reverse slope was being dug – out of sight and, as at Vimy where it stretched north and south some two miles back from the front, at the extremes of hostile artillery range. Thus extra depth would be imparted to the defence, the reserves thereby kept safe from the initial bombardment and poised for counterattacks which were carefully preconceived. The Germans, too, had formalised their artillery tactics, systematically engaging suitable forming up places if an attack seemed likely, then plastering the enemy front line once the opposing infantry came into view and finally dropping a curtain of fire in front of their own trenches to hold the enemy at arms length or isolate from their reserves those which had passed. The German artillery tended more than ever to concentrate its fire on enemy infantry instead of on counter-battery work, a shift in emphasis that was to become increasingly evident in later months.

The result of the French September attack at Vimy can be summarised in short. At a cost of 47,000 casualties

between 25th September and 11th October there was total failure. Nowhere was the crest of the Ridge reached, let alone the newly dug second line. Souchez fell and there were minor incursions in the German front line to the east of Neuville St Vaast, but even the top of the Lorette Spur at Bois en Hâche held out. Piles of dead marked a ghastly repulse. In Champagne it had been the same and only the British at Loos had made a really startling advance to the lip of the second line, until brought to a halt by the same, exact combination of hostile factors which assuredly killed any sort of infantry-based attack.

Thus the year 1915 came to an end in unavailing effort by the Allies, without a recognisable solution to any of their intractable problems. Behind the lines an infantry and artillery mass was building up with nowhere obvious to go. The Gallipoli landings had failed and there was no other means of giving direct aid to Russia where a more open front existed. All the combatants could think to do was draw deeply upon their manpower resources and turn their industry to making a juggernaut of guns supplied by mountains of shells. If 1916 was to be the year of pulverisation, significantly, it was also to be the time when German offensive intentions reverted from open warfare in the east to a slogging match in the west.

The coming of the British

So far as the French were concerned close combat took low priority once intensive offensive operations had been called off. On Vimy Ridge, as elsewhere, they elected to hold the line with field artillery (the celebrated 75mm guns) and outposts, withdrawing the bulk of their infantry into billets behind the front, strengthening the tunnels which now burrowed deep into the chalk, indulging in the absolute minimum of patrolling – pursuing, in fact, a policy of live and let live! With this the Germans were in happy accord – but with one important exception. While the French allowed their front line trenches to fall into disrepair and prosecuted only a tepid mining programme underground, the Germans dug, wired and mined with demoniac fury, fortifying the crest of Vimy Ridge more strongly than any sector of the front.

By 1916 the French army had passed the peak of its full effectiveness. True, the establishments of its front line battalions were full, but there were no more replacements. The reinforcement pool was empty and Joffre admitted that, for early 1916, the French army needed a rest, though it might then be capable of just one major effort. Therefore, reasoned Joffre at a conference of all the Allies at Chantilly in December 1915, it would be desirable for France's allies to take the strain with a series of their own offensives designed to 'wear down' the Germans. 'Wearing down' was just another word for 'nibbling' – and later would be called 'attrition', a more ugly title. Joffre, without the power to order his allies, could only persuade, but his prestige was enormous. It was agreed that each ally must play his part to the full, though attempts to coordinate every national offensive to combine as one against the Germans proved impossible to arrange. The Russians, desperately short of guns and munitions, thought they might be ready by June, the Italians by May, and the French wanted the British to attack in the winter. The new British C-in-C, General Sir Douglas Haig, was reflecting his Government's repugnance when he persuaded Joffre to reject 'wearing down', but committed the British to a limited offensive in June, somewhere between La Bassée and Ypres, as a diversion from the main Anglo-French offensive that was to be undertaken on the Somme in conjunction with the French after 1st July.

But on 21st February the Germans threw the Allied plans into disarray by launching their own version of

General Haig

'wearing down' first. At Verdun, Falkenhayn projected an onslaught on ground that was of equal emotional and strategic value to France as Vimy Ridge. It was a cold-blooded experiment by limited infantry attacks, supported by unlimited bombardment, to bleed the French army to death on ground it felt bound to defend. Coming at the nadir of the state of French reinforcements it could not have been better timed, but in selection of place it was of more than academic interest that Verdun was chosen for the experiment instead of Vimy. For Falkenhayn had rejected Arras and Vimy Ridge because, although a battle there would start on a narrow front and fatally attract the French, it must inevitably widen and absorb more divisions than Germany could spare. Moreover it would involve the British and thus cushion the effect on the French. At Verdun, where the arena was narrow, the whole business could be transacted from fixed positions and the French would be on their own.

So Vimy Ridge lay quiet, except for a couple of German raids on 8th and 21st February to distract attention from Verdun. Allied attention focussed in fascination on a titanic bombardment engulfing the Verdun forts, the slow, creeping advance of German infantry, the appalling casualties and signs of French panic when the im-

General Wilson

mensely important Fort Douaumont fell at slight cost to the Germans. Of course, the first French reaction was predictable – a request to Haig from Joffre to take over a greater length of line, to relieve more French infantry for use at Verdun, and a plea to the Allies to do all in their power to divert the German High Command. Haig was not at all ready for premature offensive action, though he would consider a hastening of the Somme offensive to June. In early March, however, he readily extended the right flank of his Third Army, under General Sir Edmund Allenby, north of Arras to include Vimy Ridge in its entirety and thus completed a link with the remainder of the British Army to the southwards. Now the British held a continuous stretch of the line from Ypres to the Somme – and could comfortably do so in the light of such gathering strength which now amounted to more than a million men in sixty-eight divisions supported by 3,500 guns.

This increase in Britain's strength was a remarkable achievement. Her army normally eschewed continental wars, being organised in time of peace to police the frontiers of her Empire. The preponderant United Kingdom element was enlisted wholly by volunteering as opposed to universal conscription which, for generations, had governed large scale recruitment by all its principal opponents and allies. From the Empire, too, came a vast concourse (largely built on militias) – the Canadian corps, composed at first of two divisions, followed by sizeable contributions from South Africa and Australia. Yet this mushroom growth by the British army created as many problems as it solved. Efficient expansion demanded a large corps of experienced, younger officers, the best of whom as it happened, were either already dead or committed to maintaining a front line force. In desperate defensives and three costly offensives the British army had learnt much, but the process of synthesising and transmitting this knowledge was inevitably slow in a conservative organisation.

In 1916, an army which rose towards its manpower peak was uneven and deficient in knowledge, and insufficiently supplied with artillery (much of whose ammunition was defective). Taken in bulk, it was a bunch of highly enthusiastic amateurs, the measure of whose willingness to fight, to learn and to die was to be epitomised by the story of their first few weeks sojourn on Vimy Ridge.

As the British arrived all was at peace and had need to be. In places the old French front line was recognisable by nothing more substantial than sandbags while in others the trench parapets were hardly bullet proof.

Below ground what at first appeared to be a comprehensive system of galleries turned out to be a veneer compromised and undermined by the far more extensive German works. Until the forward trenches could be strengthened by the infantry and fresh mining companies brought in to tackle the underground battle, the British, whose natural inclinations dictated a policy of aggression where-ever they went, had need to restrain themselves. In this period of uneasy calm a flimsy routine prevailed. A few German deserters crossed over, attempts by both sides were made at conversation (quite easy since, in places, the lines were a bare fifty yards apart) and the 18th London Regiment took an opportunity to deliver a copy of the London *Times* to their opponents.

Since General Haig's order of priorities rejected 'wearing down' operations in favour of conservation of his army's energies for an offensive in June, he might have done well to restrain the scale of operations on Vimy Ridge. But the doctrine of patrolling as a means to maintain constant ascendancy in No-Man's Land inevitably led to raid, counter-raid and persistent underground warfare. None of this would have been important, apart from a sadly lengthening casualty list, had not the British begun to win dominance of the ridge and frightened the Germans into suspecting that their tenancy was in peril. And even then nothing dramatic might have happened had not a strange coincidence juxtaposed the appointments of the two competing corps commanders.

On the British side there was Lieutenant-General Sir Henry Wilson commanding the IV Corps, who, until recently, had been Sub-Chief of the British General Staff in France and seemingly on the way to one of the highest posts, if not Chief of the Imperial General Staff itself in London. The advent of General Robertson as CIGS and Haig as C-in-C had put paid to that. His German opponent was also a man of overriding ambition, with large influence in high places and limited experience of command in the field – Falkenhayn's Deputy Chief of the General Staff, General von Freytag-Loringhoven, who had been transferred from German Liaison Officer with the Austro-Hungarian Great Headquarters to become Chief of Staff to Rupprecht. He, at his own request, was engaged for a short spell at the front, commanding IX Reserve Corps, and seeking to learn what trench warfare was about. Between the two lay a difference of attitudes governed by their current positions. The German was still on the way up, the Briton in the doldrums. Success in battle for Freytag-Loringhoven would enhance his reputation while failure could do little harm. Success for Wilson might recover his prestige, but failure might finish him for ever: he claimed to be pleased at his new appointment and sedulously fostered old connections, entertaining, among others, the Arch-

bishop of Canterbury to lunch so that he could admire the spectacle of the Lorette Spur under bombardment.

Freytag-Loringhoven had no sooner arrived than he read reports from the 163rd and 86th Regiments, which then held the narrow German enclave on the ridge. They implied that 'the posts in the front line trenches and the garrisons of the dugouts were always in danger of being buried alive. Even on the quietest night there was always the dreadful feeling that in the next moment one might die an horrible and cruel death. One stood in the front line defenceless and powerless against these fearful mine explosions . . . against this kind of warfare valour was of no avail.' It was an admission that the Germans were losing the technological war and an invitation to Freytag-Loringhoven to restore morale and win fame by the practice of retribution. Against the drift of German policy, which diverted all available men and materials into the

Above: **General Monro.** ***Below:*** **German infantry reinforces Vimy**

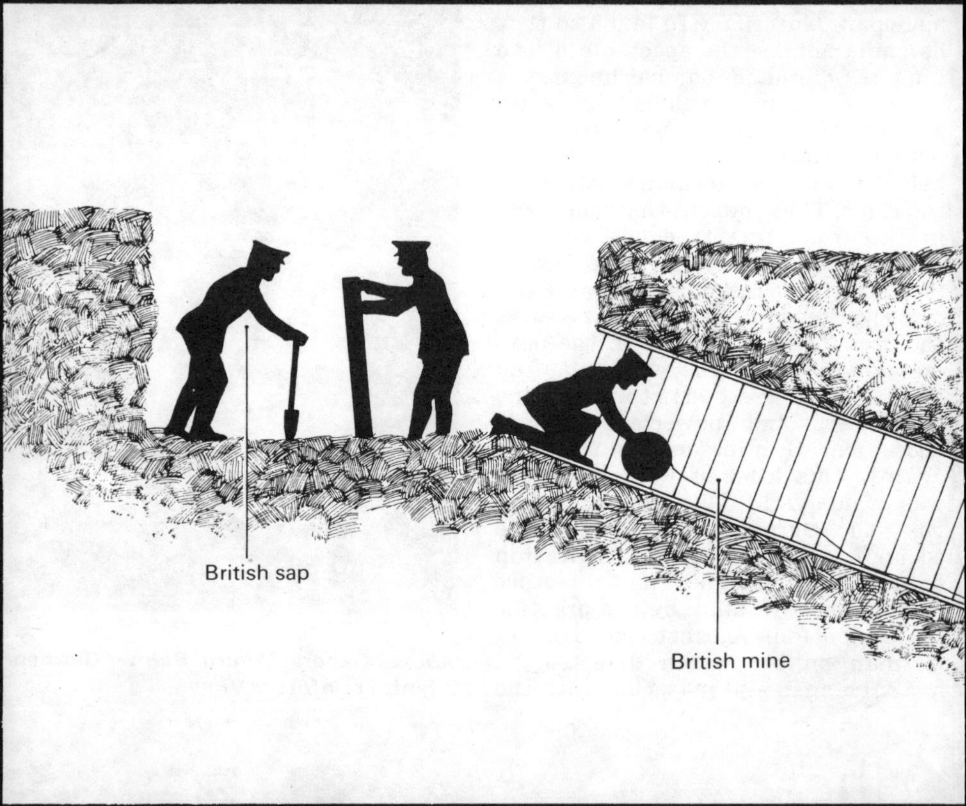

The object of mining in the First World War was to place a large amount of explosive under the enemy's front line, blowing it up at a predetermined moment and utilising the confusion so caused to occupy part of the enemy's front line at a cost in life far lower than would have been involved in a frontal assault. The technique developed in the war was to dig an open trench, known as a sap, usually in a zig-zag pattern, forward of the front line to a point as near the enemy's line as possible. This distance was usually the range to which a grenade could be thrown. From this point a tunnel or mine would be dug towards the enemy's line; the tunnel was normally lined with wood. When a position under the line had been reached, an explosive charge or mine would be placed at the end of the tunnel and tamped in such a way that most of the blast would be directed upwards into the opposition's front line trench. From the charge electric cables were laid to a safe position, and

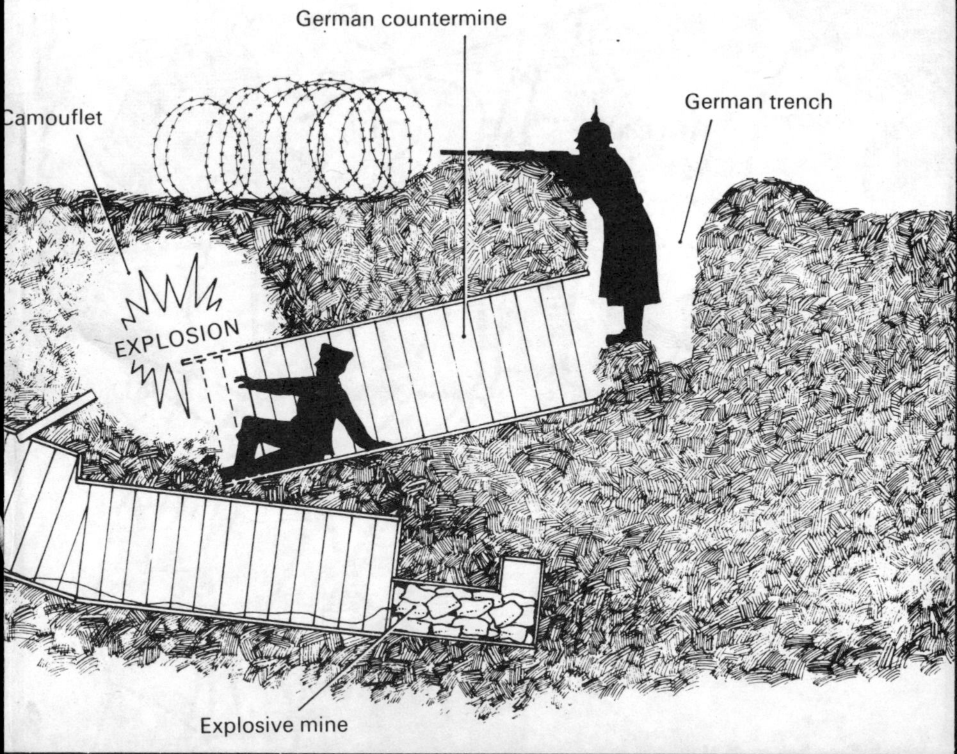

at the appointed hour the mine would be fired. The forgoing description supposes the enemy to have remained in ignorance of the mining operations. This was, however, unlikely, as he would have been listening for such activity with the use of the unaided ear or a geophone, an instrument similar to the doctor's stethoscope. If he detected mining in operation, he would dig a tunnel of his own, a countermine, and try to dig into his opponent's tunnel undetected and then destroy it. If this countermine were in turn detected, the opponent would await its arrival and then attempt to beat the enemy in a fight in the tunnel or use a device known as a camouflet. This involved pushing a long tube towards the enemy's countermine, and when it had reached a position fairly close to it, detonating an explosive charge at its tip. This was usually sufficient to cause the collapse of the countermine

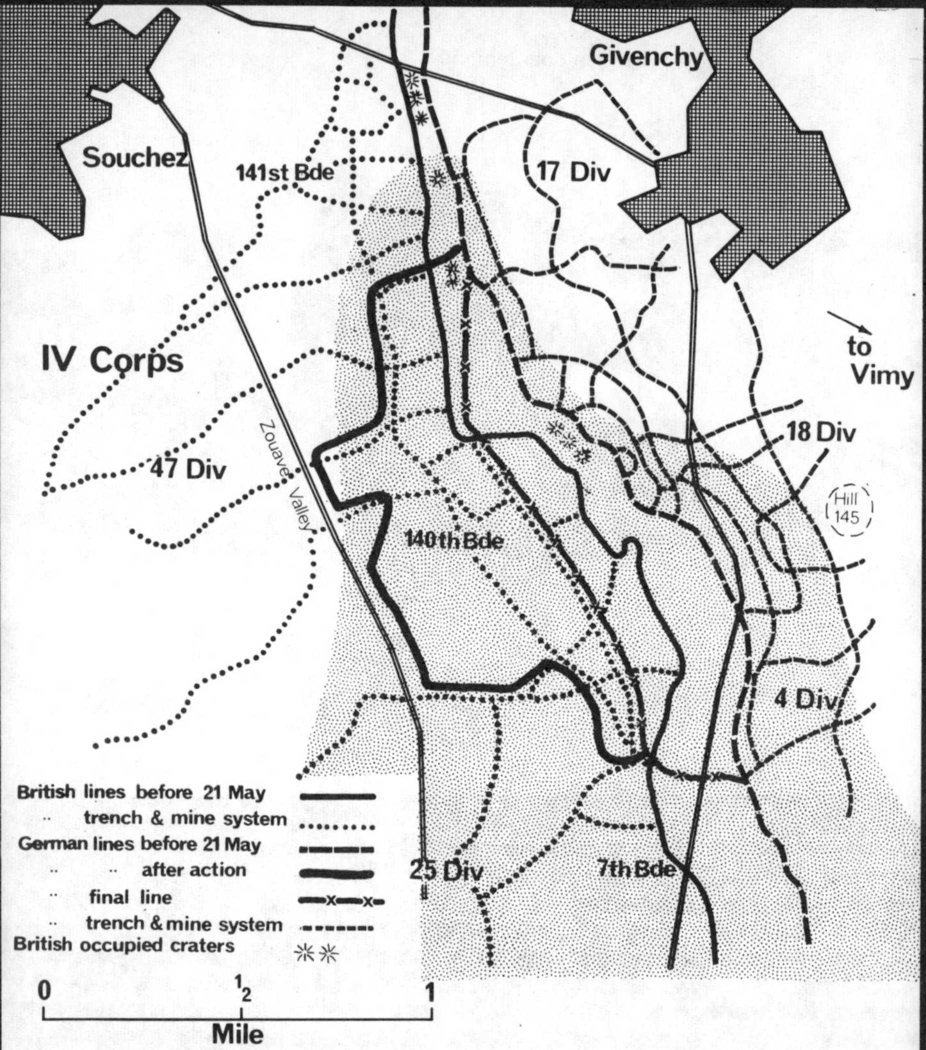

The German attack and British counterattack of May 1916

furnace at Verdun, he prevailed upon his superiors to allocate no less than eighty batteries of artillery (including six of heavy howitzers) to support the equivalent of a single division attack on a frontage of 1,600 yards – a concentration of mass achieved, what is more, without arousing British suspicion since low cloud and a clutch of lorried anti-tank guns defied British airmen and kept them at bay. At 0500 hours on 21st May German guns began a crunching bombardment which reached a peak at 1946 hours. By then, when the German infantry rushed forward, the British trenches, along with their occupants, had been torn to ribbons.

Those of the British 47th Division who stood outside the devastated area were at a loss to see what happened. The final barrage, sweeping from battery positions in rear to trenches in the front line, had raised an impenetrable cloud of smoke and dust. The Germans were firing at previously located targets to a prearranged programme and had little need to observe the fall of their shells. The British gunners, however, were deprived of a target except for scanty information from a kite-balloon observer and an RFC aircraft: their counterbattery fire imposed little restraint on the German gunners and their defensive barrage was non-existent when, at the firing of two mines, the German 86th Reserve Regiment had practically engulfed the British 140th Brigade. Thus, with little disturbance, the Germans could consolidate their objective as darkness fell, take possession of a complete set of British mine shafts (the main objective for the attack), and bring forward machineguns, timber and wire to build a new frontal system in a matter of hours. The attack had been a model of precise planning and, thus far, cheap in lives for the Germans.

With new defences patched up some 300 yards in rear, Wilson took measures to reinforce 47th Division, with 99th Brigade from 2nd Division, and to strengthen the artillery, though shortage of ammunition, not guns. was actually the problem. He then devised a counterattack since to accept the existing position would damage his reputation even if it did not imperil the line as a whole. Conference upon conference at Corps HQ followed. A plan was improvised, bedevilled by the knowledge that the Germans were rapidly fortifying their new position, that information from the front was indifferent and that Haig implied delay when he insisted upon only a 'well prepared' attack. Eventually an attack shortly before last light on the 23rd was arranged, the product of a day when the Germans, apprised by a British deserter of what was afoot, had raked the ridge systematically with gunfire.

The British bombardment began at 1925 hours and acted as the signal for German infantry in the front line prematurely to stand to and catch the full force of the shelling. Both they and the reserves, sent too early to fill gaps which as yet did not exist, were severely cut about. At the same time the German defensive fire descended upon 99th Brigade whose task it was to lead the assault. One of its battalions – 1st Berkshires – immediately lost 100 men and had its communications to the rear wrecked, with the exception of a single primitive radio set. Seeing the trenches in the process of obliteration, his men mutilated and pounded into the soil, a company commander decided against an advance since it would be suicidal. So the Berkshires stuck fast while units on their flanks got up and went forward, the one on the right gaining its objective, that on the left driven back by a counterattack. Wilson at once tried to reactivate the attack with a new and highly complex plan, instantly vetoed by the Army Commander, General Monro, who but a few hours previously had returned from leave.

The next step was to be the relief of the 47th Division and a deliberate build-up for a renewed attack on 3rd

June, plans which would demand still more artillery and impinge upon and restrict the opening phases of Haig's main offensive on the Somme. On 27th May it was Haig's turn to veto an order, stopping Monro's offensive and returning the occupants of the battered Ridge to the old game of tunnelling, raiding, watch and ward.

As a microcosm of the Western Front war the May battle on Vimy Ridge was the acme of truth, a battle generated from accumulating external pressures brought to the boil by the selfish ambition of the two senior commanders. It is argued that decisions to cause nearly 3,000 casualties, such as Freytag-Loringhoven or Wilson had taken, were without compassion. But both officers, Wilson in particular, regularly visited the front line and possessed insight into the conditions of the fighting men. But in the final analysis of the mechanism of command as a function of human endeavour, they had no option other than to divorce themselves from the cruel realities of an assault, driving their gunners to intensify their efforts to make the front line utterly untenable to frail human beings. Abject terror mixed with the stern demands of duty and the clash of loyalty such as would transfix the men in 99th Brigade who advanced, and those who declined to do so, can only be properly understood by somebody who has actually walked deliberately into a hail of lethal, flying metal. People may sometimes picture themselves in the situation of a man waiting execution and have, in conscience in many countries, outlawed the death sentence. In war the feeling of inevitability is attenuated by the degree of hope in a man's breast as he calculates the factors in chance of survival, balancing the enemy's power against his own side's plan and prowess. In the First World War the chances of survival for front line infantrymen were abysmally low and many were placed in the position of the man

The Germans dug in on the Ridge

The knife edge

awaiting execution. On climbing out of a trench the infantryman always put to extreme hazard that most precious and irredeemable thing in the world – his life. It is easy to forget that, in any operation of war – be it the grand scale offensive which hits the news headlines or the smallest patrol which receives no mention – those involved are engaged in the most profound operation.

So Haig brought a halt to the carnage on the Ridge though not without second thoughts, thoughts which turned to the day when he might *have* to take possession either for the ground's local military value or as the essential cornerstone to some important venture. Therefore with his veto also came instructions to IV Corps to study plans for the conclusive acquisition of Vimy Ridge.

British gunners, hampered by lack of ammunition

By the end of 1916, each side had suffered total casualties surpassing the million mark at Verdun, on the Somme and in other theatres of war. Only the undertaker (when he could find something recognizable to bury) had been the winner, for in the west territorial and strategic gains had been minimal while in the east great advances by the Russians had stopped short of a conclusion. Each army had forfeited the cream of its manpower and the best of its well-trained regulars and veterans of the earlier campaigns. Combat techniques drifted in a limbo of unoriginality in which soldiers' ideas, lacking subtlety, were channelled into an orgy of intensifying destruction. The virtue of surprise to win a psychological advantage had been cast aside and in its place stood brute force – 'improved' artillery techniques such as could now concentrate, switch and aim the fire of hundreds of guns by something approaching remote control at the call of a handful of controllers impersonally picking targets off the map.

The 'nerveless' weapons such as machine-guns were also extending their repertoire, the original 'heavy type' burgeoning out as a fire support weapon in attack, using barrage methods; the new, lighter versions carried everywhere by assaulting infantry – but each, in the end, contributing more to defence than to attack. To some extent artillery might subjugate the nerveless weapons, cut gaps in the wire and silence enemy artillery, but total dominance by gunfire demanded so vast an outlay as to abrogate all chances of total surprise. In any case it only required a single surviving machine-gun to stop an infantry company or wipe out an entire regiment of cavalry.

Somewhat tentatively in 1916 the British had tried an expedient to break the deadlock – a weapon with the glimmer of originality in its make-up. They experimented with a new device that would combine armoured protection with mobility in which its crew could drive reasonably safely through the wire to aim immediate gunfire at the enemy trenches. These 'tanks', some three dozen of which saw hesitant action for the first time in the latter stages of the Somme battle without appreciably affecting its outcome. But the British and Canadian infantry who noticed their effect on terror-struck Germans welcomed them, even if the British and German General Staffs harboured strict reservations as to their future as a war winning weapon. So while the British went on building a few tanks, along with the French who had already started a larger construction programme of their own, the main stream of industrial effort poured forth guns and still more guns along with millions of tons of ammunition.

Perhaps the nearest thing to a war winning campaign had been fought in Russia where General Brusilov's offensive had overrun Austro-Hungarian Armies and advanced to the borders of Rumania just as that country was about to plunge into war on the Allied side. The Rumanians were crushed – their overthrow the sole Central Powers' success that gloomy year of frustration – but Brusilov's offensive died from exhaustion. Nevertheless, the Germans were compelled to worry all the more about their closest allies, the Austro-Hungarians, when the Emporor Franz Joseph died in December 1916 to be succeeded by his son Karl, whose heart was set on peace.

In August the winning partnership of Hindenburg and Ludendorff had replaced Falkenhayn. The failure at Verdun where the 'mincing machine' had been stopped as the Anglo-French offensive sucked his last reserves into the vortex of the Somme, had been his undoing. Ludendorff drew the conclusion that the Central Powers were no longer in a condition for offensive action on land, that severe restrictions would have to be placed on offensive action, both on the Eastern and Western Fronts, in order to restore the army's wellbeing and create a cen-

The new German team, Hindenburg and Ludendorff

tral reserve. He figured that the best chance of reaching a swift and final decision, favourable to Germany, was the institution of an unlimited submarine campaign designed to starve Britain into submission. Yet he figured only loosely. When it came to land warfare Ludendorff was capable of the most sophisticated calculations that took account of diverse factors of morale and political expediency. His evolving concept of shortening the Western Front by withdrawing into a rearward fortified zone from the exposed salients which, over two years, had been driven haphazard into France, was to be carefully considered and efficiently executed. Strategic withdrawals to a prepared line were common in the history of war and, in any case, the work that began on what was to be called the 'Hindenburg Line', stretching from Arras to Vailly in the south, was at this stage merely a precautionary measure. Plans for its occupation after a deliberate withdrawal were left in the realms of conjecture.

Unlimited submarine warfare, however, was an uncalculated risk with-

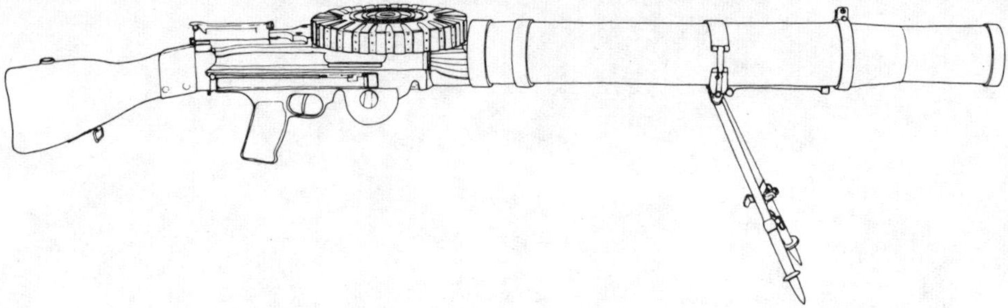

The Lewis Mk I light machine gun. This was the standard light machine gun used by the British army in the First World War. Designed by an American, Colonel Isaac Newton Lewis, the gun was not adopted by the US Army, so Lewis brought the design to Europe, where quantity production was initiated by the Belgians. The main advantages of the weapon were its light weight and consequently its portability. Its disadvantage was the relative weakness of the mechanism, and its proneness to stoppages when only slightly dirty. *Calibre:* .303-inch. *System of operation:* Gas, automatic only. *Weight:* 27lbs. *Length overall:* 50.5 inches. *Barrel length:* 26.04 inches. *Feed:* 47 round drum. *Muzzle velocity:* 2,440 feet per second. *Coolant:* Air

out precedent in history. There was a total lack of scientific data to prove that the sea lanes that led to Britain from all over the world (but chiefly from America and Canada) could be cut. There was no guarantee that submarines could not be defeated or evaded. Moreover there was the appalling risk, in the light of previous United States' reaction to uninhibited sinking of merchant ships, that underwater war would bring the USA into the struggle on the Allied side. The German Admiralty's unsupported statistical claim that, within six months, the submarines would decide the issue so thoroughly that the USA would be isolated from intervention in Europe, was indefensible. The Germans were aware that, in 1917, the Americans could offer nothing better than a vast potential in manpower, materials and industrial capacity but, that apart, had nothing for immediate use in the battle, except the US Navy, and that would be least in demand due to the eclipse of the German Fleet by the British at the Battle of Jutland in 1916. Even so, holding a relatively weak political and military hand, the Germans bid as if from strength on the assumption that the submarine was a trump card. Their so-called 'Peace Proposals', guarded from close public examination, were the demands of a victorious nation and bound to be rejected by the Allies.

By contrast the Allies, still comparatively secure on the ocean's surface and inexorably if slowly suffocating the Central Powers by blockade, saw in land warfare the only hope of a quick solution to the war before their people's patience ran out. In November 1916 Joffre, in consultation with Haig, settled upon the continuance of French offensive operations in 1917 between the Rivers Oise and Somme (plus a secondary attack on the River Aisne) while the British attacked between Bapaume and Vimy. The French army was in decline while the British was reaching the peak of its development, well supplied with artillery and amply backed by reserves now that industrial output had been rationalised and conscription introduced. When meeting Joffre's desires Haig also stipulated an offensive in Flanders to satisfy British Admiralty requirements for the capture of Ostend and Zeebrugge as a curb to German U-Boat activities. With this Joffre fell into accord, as he so frequently did with the stubborn yet sympathetic Haig.

But by 26th December Joffre's previously unchallenged power had evaporated under a welter of French political dissatisfaction with his lack of measurable progress in bringing the war to an end. Cornered by the desperation of their sacrifices in their own territory the French now searched for a panacea and found it, so they thought, in the ideas of one man who had won lightning, aggressive successes at Verdun. For while Pétain was regarded as the saviour of Verdun, in a strictly defensive mien, it was General Robert Nivelle, whose dramatic ripostes to recapture Fort Douaumont in October, and the heights beyond it in December, who took their imagination as 'the general with the secret of victory'. Nivelle was indeed possessed of abundant enthusiasm and carried an aura of conviction as he crested the wave with a charm which beguiled the politicians and seems even to have impressed Haig. He was quite the opposite of the dour and domineering Joffre and he possessed the advantage of fluent conversation in English when communicating with his principal ally. His methods would be different too.

The outline plan proposed by Nivelle, and largely accepted by Haig in January, bore only a passing resemblance to the original evolved by Joffre. There was to be a complete change in emphasis, for while Joffre had been driven by two years hard experience to adopt the strategy of 'attrition' – pushing towards random strategic objectives as they revealed themselves – Nivelle, on the basis of two miniature and easy successes in October and December as a mere army commander, maintained his long-held faith in the attack *à outrance* directed towards an all-embracing strategic goal. Joffre had envisaged joint Anglo-French operations. Nivelle relegated the British attack between Bapaume and Vimy to a subordinate place in a scheme dominated by the French army, which would first deliver an attack on the Oise as a preliminary to the main rupture of the German lines across the Aisne. The French mass of manoeuvre would hurl itself northwards, across the German line of retreat, to link with the British somewhere between St Quentin and Cambrai, before turning eastward, in unison with its ally, in pursuit of a beaten enemy. All this Haig welcomed but with the canny stipulation that, if Nivelle failed, those British troops allotted should be withdrawn to play their part in his favourite Flanders offensive. Thus Haig preserved the autonomy of the British army at a time when Briand and Lloyd George (the French and British Prime Ministers) were proposing the creation of an Allied HQ with Nivelle as Supreme Commander-in-Chief. This Haig, along with Robertson the British CIGS, rejected in a fury, carrying their point with the threat that 'they would rather be tried by Court Martial than betray the army by agreeing to its being placed under the French.' Yet Nivelle was thinking on the right lines even if his timing was adrift and his prestige lower than that of Joffre – and he also achieved a measure of official autonomy better than anything enjoyed by Joffre.

Moreover, when it came to tactics, Nivelle's ideas were actually well in advance of the 1914 concept of 'man over material'. As cavalryman turned artilleryman, his faith revolved primarily on the scientific demolition of the enemy position by gunfire. Only then could the pursuit in depth be launched. These methods Nivelle had shown as feasible on a small scale, providing the enemy continued to align his mass in the immediate forward zone. In these circumstances Nivelle merely substituted the killing power of artillery for what was once considered the prerogative of infantry and cavalry.

But Ludendorff, in love with his strategy of inflexible defence, adopted revised and flexible tactics to counter the effects of the hurricane bombardments upon which Nivelle depended for everything. Henceforward the German front would be thinly held, resistance being developed progressively in depth, within a prepared 'battle zone' some 1,500 to 2,000 yards behind outposts. In this battle zone the interplay of intense artillery fire, linked to counteraction by mobile reserves, would bring the enemy to a halt on ground of the defenders choosing. As many reserves as possible would be stationed beyond the reach of artillery fire. Rigid linear tactics of mass, such as permeated infantry doctrine until 1916, now gave way to 'group tactics' in which small parties would be permitted freedom of manoeuvre within certain prescribed limits. Each man's initiative was to be exploited and his morale enhanced by Ludendorff's idea that the infantryman need no longer fight on the basis 'Here I must stand or fall' – and in this way fears that a total strategic offensive would be largely destructive of morale were dissipated. The new Hindenburg Line was built to the measure of these tactics, but, even if its fortifications were ready before spring, the minds of the men who would occupy them remained cramped by past restrictive drills that could not be converted overnight to expansive improvisations such as defence in depth required. Thus the year 1917 began with the German army in a state of transition and uncertainty as fundamental to its future performance as would be the shift of German policy, from a land to a maritime emphasis, on the future of Germany as a nation.

Practically ignorant of developments behind the German lines in a winter notorious for its dreadful weather – thick fog, heavy cloud and rain, fierce blizzards and hard freeze – the Anglo-French armies made ready for Nivelle's *coup de grâce*. Haig calculated that his force would be at its peak in May and he expected an encouraging outcome of the attack to be launched at Arras. In conference he resisted Nivelle's suggestion that, since the main British thrust should be in the direction of Cambrai, the Heights of Vimy Ridge could be omitted from the scheme. Haig was his own master, engaged in launching an offensive of great complexity by four armies – the largest campaign ever undertaken by a British force. He would have his way and include the Ridge in his plan because it gave flank protection and an unrivalled view of the Plain of Douai. Nor was he unduly impressed by the report of 7th July 1916 from Monro's First Army stating that an attack on the ridge was 'not possible unless the enemy is showing signs of weakness'.

Haig's original orders were for First Army (now under the command of General Sir Henry Horne) to prepare the capture of Vimy Ridge, employing a small part of the I British Corps on the left to take the Bois en Hâche and the whole of Canadian Corps to subdue the ridge from between Bois de Givenchy and Bois de Farbus. The remainder of the ridge, where it fell away south to the Scarpe, would be the responsibility of XVIII Corps in Allenby's Third Army, the principal formation whose chief task it also was to break out east of Arras, to the south of the Scarpe, and lunge for a junction at Cambrai with the French as they approached from the south. Meanwhile General Sir Hubert Gough's Fifth Army was to carry out a much smaller offensive directed upon Achiet le Grand, sandwiched between the attack of General Sir Henry Rawlinson's Fourth Army towards Bapaume. Thus Haig staked everything upon the success of Allenby at Arras: the attacks against Vimy Ridge to the north of Arras and against Bapaume, away to the south, were only meant to seize important ground and widen the shoulders of the deep salient Allenby was to create.

Yet the assault against Vimy Ridge loomed largest in everybody's estimation and in consequence the history of

General Horne

Above: The nightly battles of patrols and working parties. *Below:* Hot food for the men in the trenches. *Right:* General Byng

the main Allied offensive, which was set to start on 8th April, has tended to become forgotten. Not unnaturally this slight warping of historical perspective is most noticeable in Canada. Many Canadians, at the time and after the assault, were unaware that their principal task was buttress to a far larger edifice. The reasons for this state of affairs are fairly obvious. Vimy Ridge had a reputation for impregnability. Merely to attempt its reduction was to challenge the impossible. But, once achieved, the blush of triumph, added to the incomparable advantage of holding such dominating ground, would be intoxicating. This, in the eyes of the world (and sedulously fostered by Canadian propagandists) would be the stark manifestation of Canadian independence written plain for all to see by the first major independent operation by the complete Canadian Corps of four divisions. No matter that the Corps commander was a Britisher (Lieutenant-General Sir Julian Byng), or that much of the heavy artillery upon which so much depended, was British. This understandably and demonstrably, was going to be Canada's very own show.

It was indeed a remarkable achievement that in just two and a half years Canada could put such a formidable army in the field. In 1914 the nation's regular element had been but 3,110 men and 684 horses strong, the part-time Militia 55,000. Of guns there were only 200 modern types (barely enough for two divisions), of transport little

A wounded survivor from a patrol crawls in

enough, while even personal clothing and equipment was in short supply and out of date. Yet in the midst of an immediate and vast expansion by an influx of volunteers, a first convoy of men and material was being assembled at the dockside in conditions of trial, error and utter chaos, sailing for the United Kingdom on 2nd October 1914. By February 1915 Canadian troops were experiencing their first taste of the front line and in April the 1st Division played its memorable part in stemming the rout of the French at Ypres during the first gas attack. Thereafter it expanded to a corps of two divisions, which took part in the Battle of the Somme, and redoubled to the four divisions which entered the line at Vimy Ridge in October 1916. Its increase was in parallel with its progress in learning a new and painful art of war. Step by step with the British, largely dependent on other nations' guns for medium and heavy support and almost invariably integrated (as of previous policy) with a minimum of ceremony into British plans, the Canadian army acted virtually as an integral part of the British army. But forever there seethed the ambition of a healthy child who seeks to shake off the influence of its parent, and so the story of Canada's army in the First World War is that of struggle to do better than the British army – and to do it their way.

The Hindenburg Line

The winter of 1916/17 was the hardest and most squalid of the war. Where months of incessant bombardment had ravaged the land, wrecking drainage systems and levelling the surrounding trees and buildings, men scraped for survival in a welter of freezing stagnant water, mud and carrion. Horror abounded. On the warmer days the sickly smell from unburied dead would compete to poison the atmosphere with rancid gas that hung heavily in hollows and at the bottom of trenches. In the sticky slough a foot placed carelessly on some yielding hummock might at any moment reveal nauseating corruption – putrefaction distilled such as shattered men's senses. Enduring conditions like these it was hardly surprising that an incapacitating wound – sometimes self-inflicted – became welcome. Better that than, perhaps, temporary rest giving periodic relief from the line or a spell in hospital suffering from one of the popular ailments such as trench foot or bronchitis – always dreading the day of return to the line. Freeze or snow – as it did for most of that winter – there was never respite from the fear of death by bullet, shell or even exposure to the elements. There was, however, a degree of choice in the shelter to be found – better to be underground in a cave up on Vimy Ridge or in Arras than waist deep in the mud of a trench down by the Scarpe.

Arras provided the classic example of the truly 'desirable' fortress. Here the cellars, built by generations of burgesses for purposes of trade and war, could house an army while the discovery that the sewers, conforming to the course of the Crinchon Stream, passed close to a number of ancient caves beyond the eastern outskirts of the city, gave impetus to an elaborate new project. For it was found to be relatively easy to link the cellars to the sewers, and thence to the caves and, at selected points, tunnel beneath the German lines to give secret access to the surface *behind* their forward positions. Throughout the winter of 1917 this work went ahead and came eventually to provide safe accommodation for over 24,000 men, administrative centres and hospitals – all fitted with electricity, ventilation and drainage besides a sally port under the enemy lines.

Tunnelling on Vimy Ridge was an all-consuming occupation though its ramifications fell short in sophistication of those in the environs of Arras. Throughout the summer of 1916 the British sappers, by sheer guts and persistence, had won total domination over the Germans in the underground war. Indeed by September the latter had virtually conceded defeat, leaving the British free to develop an incomparable network of covered approaches leading forward from far to the rear up to and, in places, beyond the front line, with exits in the middle of No-Man's Land. Here, too, the complete fabric of army command, control and administration, lay beneath

ground level and it was this complex system that was taken over and improved by the Canadians in October 1916. They dwelt mainly in safety with only the minimum number of men to keep watch in the trenches on the surface. But just behind the front line lived the Canadian gunners, existing in worse squalor than some of their infantry compatriots, in conditions described by one of their number, Frank Lomax.

'The gunners lived in the old rat-infested French dug-outs, barely kept alive by Huntley and Palmer's No 4 biscuits, almost as tough as plywood, and a small ration of bully beef. Water was obtained by melting snow over a meagre wood fire. About once a week one loaf of bread was issued for division among ten men. It was frozen solid and had to be cut with a wood saw. The men were thoroughly lousy, unwashed and with their physical strength well below par.' In a state of abject degradation men turned to

Above: General Allenby. *Below:* The blue forest of wire

bizarre pastimes to ease the boredom which mostly prevailed. Describing a gun pit located in Neuville St Vaast cemetery, Lomax goes on: 'In one corner was an emergent head with long flaxen tresses and from the walls pairs of feet and thigh bones protruded. The ghoulish surroundings heightened the boys' sense of humour. On arrival for successive stages of the job they stroked the flaxen tresses and hung their tin lids on pulled out thigh bones.'

These gunners dictated play at the front, whether men stayed below cover or emerged to give battle. Every day and most of each night both sides' guns went on the rampage, harassing rearward areas and each other, pummelling the barbed wire entanglements to prevent repairs being made by quaking working parties. Raids were frequent, costly and most times senseless. In one particular fortnight the Canadians suffered 1,400 casualties: in a notorious raid on Point 145 they lost 687. It all helped maintain the atmosphere of Hell on Earth in sub-zero temperatures. One Canadian soldier describes a typical raid: 'Just as we started out the Germans left their trenches to attack our line. We were right in No-Man's Land with our barrage between the Germans and their trench and their barrage between us and our trench. That was the only time I used a bayonet on a live target. I can still see the poor devil's face when he got it.'

Bayonet fights, in fact, were relatively unusual events in this war when even accurate rifle shooting fell steadily into decline. There was no longer the prewar emphasis on precise target practice aimed to kill a man at long range. Infantry shooting resolved itself into the hasty discharge of a stream of metal, preferably from behind cover, in the general direction of the target, using a machinegun rather than the rifle if possible. Only the specially trained snipers took pride in drawing a steady bead for the single, deadly shot. In most cases the infantry soldiers, when at last they got to close quarters, preferred to use the grenade as a more impersonal and certain method of killing or immobilising several men at once.

Frequently the individual German infantryman, the equal of his opponents in personal prowess, was more effective due to superior organisation and direction. Take away that better direction, however, and his morale could collapse as rapidly – perhaps more rapidly – than that of any other soldier. And it was the threatened collapse of infantry morale which, exemplified by a new-found willingness to give up and surrender on call, mainly induced Ludendorff to authorise a staged withdrawal to the Hindenburg Line. The actual removal or destruction of stores was to begin on 9th February, the first so-called 'Marching Day' was 16th February, and the operation was to be complete by 16th March – though in fact it continued in places until 5th April.

The utmost thoroughness went into preparations designed not only to deceive the Allies of what impended and to remove the troops and as much material as possible to safety, but also, as part of a policy of incomparable and absolute destruction, to obliterate everything that stood within the zone to be evacuated. Of civilians to be left behind there were only to be useless mouths – a few thousand elderly folk, women and children. Trees were to be felled, buildings razed, roads cratered, bridges destroyed – everything flattened or made useless – a policy as repugnant to many Germans as it was horrifying to the Allied soldiers who cautiously entered this man-made desert on the heels of the German rearguard. A policy which also brought Rupprecht (now commanding the Army Group that stretched from the Oise to the North Sea) to the verge of resignation at a time when he looked upon the future with deepest gloom. He, along

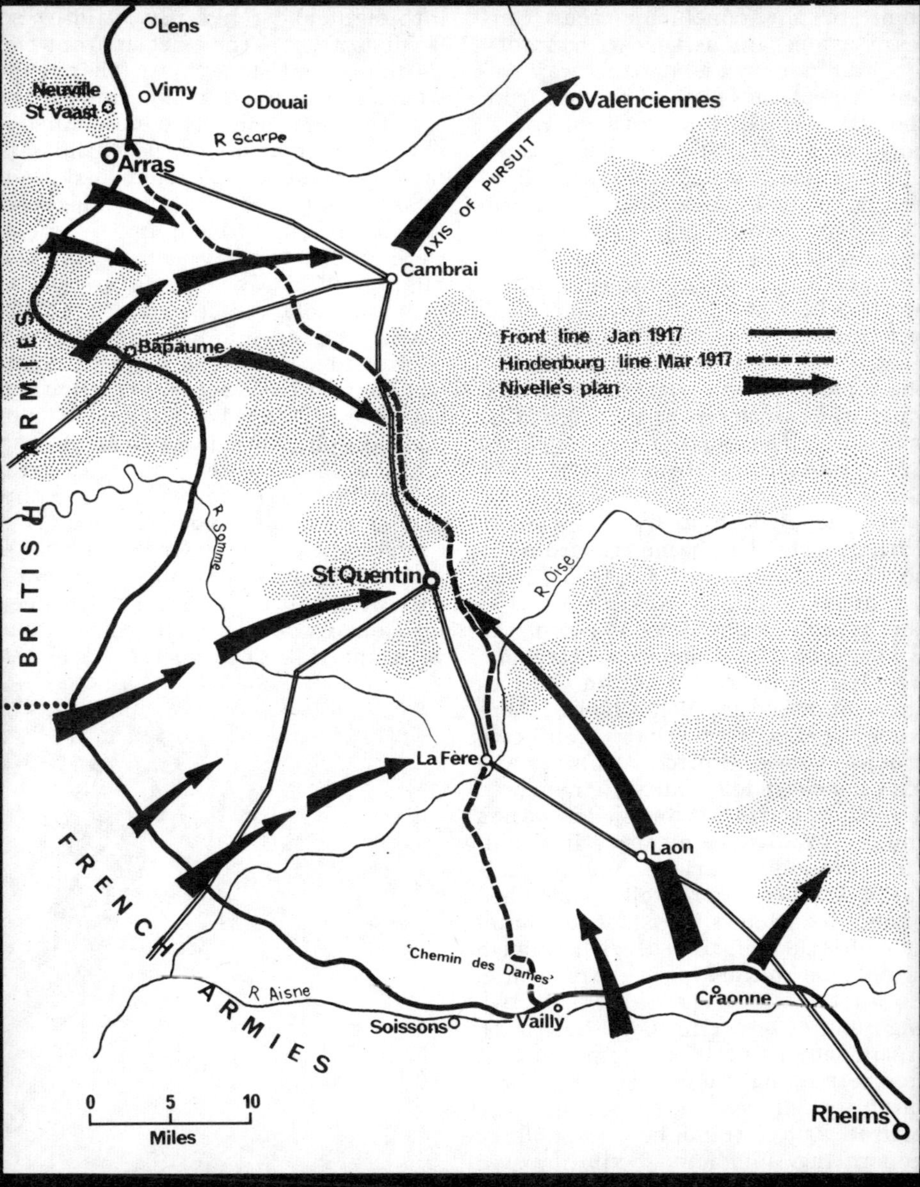

The retreat to the Hindenburg Line and Nivelle's plan for a major offensive in 1917

with the German Crown Prince, had come to the conclusion that Germany's hopes lay neither with victory on land nor by submarine warfare. Only the withdrawal of Russia from the war seemed to offer the slightest hope of relief for an overstrained German army that badly needed to revert to a one-front war. Then, on 12th March, everything went into the melting-pot as, with startling suddenness, Russia broke into Revolution and the Tsar was deposed. Even if this left Russia officially committed to hostilities it undoubtedly slackened the tension on the Eastern Front and gave the German army breathing space and the opportunity to withdraw additional formations into reserve.

To the British army the sudden withdrawal of German forces from the southern portion of their front, from the hinge at Tillois opposite Arras to the extreme right flank north of the River Avre, was a shocking interlude. Apart from its revelation of German thoroughness in demolition there came a discovery that their own troops, whose limited training and experience had inured them to trench warfare, were at a loss when invited to advance at speed in conditions of mobile warfare. Against skilfully trained and well positioned enemy rearguards they lacked a practiced battle drill to deal with ambush situations and advanced guard action. So what would be the result if, following a major breakthrough at Arras in April, they had the task of pursuing a fast retreating enemy? To some there might seem reason to suspect the citizen army would be incapable of generating sufficient flexibility and thrust in the open warfare for which they all yearned.

Haste in following up the German withdrawal was of the essence, particularly to the right flank formations of Third Army and the entire Fifth Army, on Third Army's right, if they were to readjust and shift everything forward before starting the battering of the Hindenburg Line when it came into sight and range. By building so far distant from the existing front the Germans had done more than construct a line in seclusion, unimpeded by fire; they had introduced an obscure conundrum to potential attackers even though they had been unable wholly to conceal its secrets. For while the French in the south were only vaguely aware of the alignment, let alone the nature, of the new obstacle (as labour from Germany, Belgium and Russian prisoners of war dug, wired and built throughout that terrible winter) the British, supplied with a generous collection of photographs, taken at fearful risk and cost by the RFC, had gleaned a pretty thorough picture of its extent and details. This part of the Flying Corps' work was indeed memorable since the pilots were forced to navigate with only rudimentary aids, deep into enemy territory in thick cloud with the risk of almost certain des-

truction if once they were caught by the superior German fighters. They flew, what was more, straight across the door-step of the celebrated Richthofen Staffel at Douai, adding numerous contributions to his score and that of his followers.

Yet even with clear knowledge of the new entrenchments it could not be certain that the Germans would retire into them across the entire Western Front or just occupy the sector to the south of Arras. Either way the preparations for the Allied offensive could be nullified, though, as it was, only the offensives on the Oise and Somme were actually still-born. North of the Scarpe, however, it soon became evident that the German Sixth Army under General von Falkenhausen was staying put. Vimy Ridge was to be held, its garrison perched on the rim of eternity. So Nivelle's main plan remained inviolate since Haig, with certain adjustments, could readily attack an enemy in position at Arras

Above: Richtofen. *Below:* A German casualty of the air war

as the French tackled the Germans on the north bank of the Aisne on the Chemin des Dames. Haig's revised plan, issued on 26th March, told First Army to capture Vimy Ridge as hitherto, but mentioned the allocation of an additional corps to exploit success in the direction of Douai – an escalation of First Army's original role above that of flank guard. Nevertheless, it must be emphasised that very little thought seems to have been given to this new development, largely because the rigidity and complexity of artillery methods were to rule against a flexible exploitation. Third Army continued to hold pride of place as the main striking force while Fifth Army was ordered to converge as fast as possible on its right to exert pressure towards Quéant and thus prop Third Army's

General Nivelle

right shoulder as it advanced. Fourth Army – its offensive pre-empted – was merely to follow the retiring Germans to their stopping place in the Hindenburg Line.

Tension mounted high as the final adjustments to the plan were made, as conglomerations of ammunition and stores accumulated behind the assault positions and formations emerged from winter quarters to limber up for battle. Artillery from both sides raised the tempo of their exchanges, for while Third Army's principal bombardment was not due to open until 4th April, that against Vimy Ridge by the Canadian Corps was to begin on 20th March, starting what the Germans came to call 'the Week of Suffering'. From then on Vimy Ridge was to rock incessantly in a sea of erupting flame, smoke and broken earth until the issue was decided.

Above: **After the deluge: transport stuck in the mud**
Below: **General Falkenhausen**

The guns take charge

Along twenty miles of trench line no less than fifteen infantry divisions were to be used in the assault by First and Third Armies, backed up by seven more in immediate reserve together with three cavalry divisions. In addition four more infantry, plus a cavalry division, were to operate on the right flank under Fifth Army while others could be fed from reserve or the flanks should Haig feel the need. These divisions were mainly concentrated against Vimy Ridge and along a short frontage of a mere five miles east of Arras, a gathering of flesh and blood which had not the slightest chance of advancing if the opposition provided by eleven German divisions was not previously blotted out. Outright bravery on its own merits might well carry infantry parties into the German front line but even this could not sustain them beyond. For the accomplishment of a breakthrough, apart from artillery, there existed only a few tanks – some sixty in number – which might be of direct assistance, but sheer unreliability and shortage of numbers undermined their claim to offer anything better than local assistance. Tanks used in mass on a narrow frontage had been proposed and rejected by commanders and staffs who disliked gambling upon unproven weapons.

15-inch howitzer, instrument of pulverisation

Allocation of Artillery 9th April 1917

First Army mostly with Canadian corps

artillery weapons	weight of shell in pounds	First Army	Third Army
18 pounder	18.5	548	858
4.5 – inch howitzer	35	174	276
60 pounder	55	114	144
6 – inch howitzer	100	144	220
6 – inch gun	100	16	24
8 – inch howitzer	200	40	84
9.2 – inch howitzer	290	56	92
9.2 – inch gun	380	NIL	2
12 – inch howitzer	850	4	13
12 – inch gun	850	NIL	2
18 – inch howitzer	1400	3	5

8-inch howitzer

Nevertheless, the experience gained by the tanks on the Somme was capitalised to some extent: greater care would be taken in preparing them for action and such concentration as was possible aimed south of the Scarpe. There the majority of the tanks were to be used at the outset with the added contingency of grouping them for limited exploitation towards Monchy le Preux on the second day.

So it was to be upon the guns that all rested, the battle to be won or lost by the power and ability of British and German gunners to obliterate each other, to fling open or lock shut the battlefield to infantry and cavalry. Never before had the technique of applying such enormous fire-power grown so sophisticated or complex. The table shows the vast number of guns involved along with the weight of each gun's shell, while some notion of the scale of output can be gained from the realisation that, for the attack on Vimy Ridge alone, no less than 42,609 tons of artillery ammunition were allocated in bulk in addition to a further daily allotment of 2,465 tons. Dumping of this stupendous load of material by the train, lorry and wagon load had begun in January and continued in parallel with vast accumulations of engineer's stores and concentrations of men and horses – all demanding a colossal ancillary programme of rail and road construction along with the building of gun pits, shelters and depôts. Arras and the surrounding countryside, having previously been partially denuded of its indigenous population, now acquired a vast new temporary urbanisation such as overstrained all the existing services, particularly the local water supply. And all this increase took place in the worst of winters and mostly by night.

To create and manipulate so vast and complex a programme new deities and organisations had to be created to

General Birch

act as advisors and executives to overburdened senior commanders. Vying for power with the omnipotent General Staff, a chief artillery advisor, a so-called Major-General Royal Artillery (MGRA), had been appointed to Haig. And from GHQ this officer, Major-General Noel Birch, established a network of power running through MGRAs at army HQs to similar functionaries at corps, division, brigade and battalion level, reaching forward to the meanest Forward Observation Officer crouched at the end of a telephone beside his infantry comrades in the dirtiest front line trench. For all external purposes the traditional commanders and staffs of cavalry and infantry formations would lay the central plans for attack. In practice, the artillery commanders and staff who had been superimposed upon the old establishments, would virtually dictate policy. In their immensity they were now omnipotent. In support of Canadian Corps alone were 1st and 2nd Canadian Heavy Artillery Groups and the following British Heavy Artillery Groups: XIII, XVIII, XXVI, XLIV, LXX and LXXVI comprising batteries of all the bigger calibres. Historians often forget to mention these enormously powerful formations by name, but without them in 1917 armies were virtually impotent. Quite obviously, therefore, the officers who came to control and match these massive concentrations to the involved and uncertain movements of advancing divisions had to

Naval gun

be educated men of the highest calibre. They were the rising generation of technologists who had come to dominate the war. Little enough credit has been paid them for their achievement, just as, often enough, they escaped castigation behind their commanders' coat-tails when things went wrong.

This organisation, having accumulated the ammunition, had then to unload it upon German targets as varied in nature as the types of gun and shell provided. Mostly the job was to be done by day, to allow adequate observation and photography of the results. Night firing took place only for the harassment of German reliefs entering the line, of resupply missions and parties endeavouring to repair the day's destruction. Working systematically from front to rear, mortars and 18-pounders were to destroy wire entanglements along with the forward trench system, each battery concentrating its fire on specific targets rather than attempting the general (and invariably less effective) disruption of an area. 4.5-inch and 6-inch howitzers were to superimpose their plunging fire on the flat trajectory output of 18-pounders blasting the front line trenches. The 60-pounders were to sweep communication trenches, light railways and billets behind the front line. For the 8- and 9.2-inch pieces, with their heavier shells, was reserved the vital task of counter-

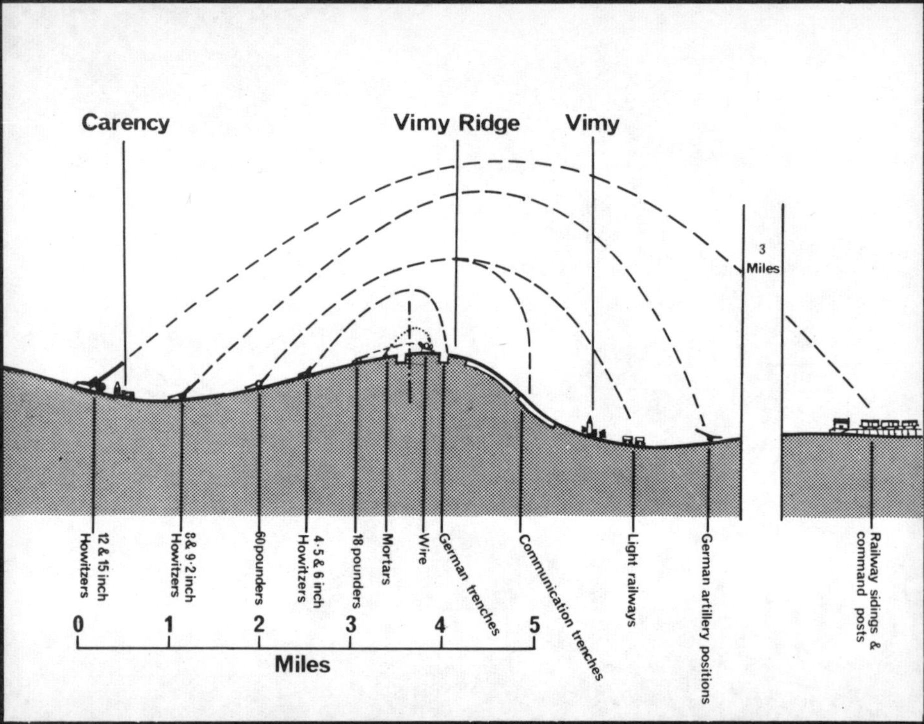

British artillery and its objectives during the Vimy offensive. Each gun matched by range and nature to appropriate targets

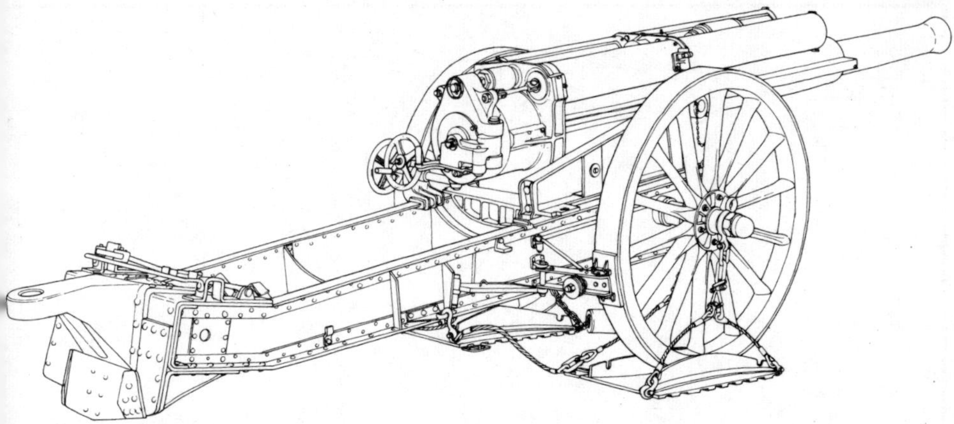

The British 60-pounder gun, Mark I. ***Weight of shell:*** **60lbs.** ***Weight of carriage with gun:*** **58cwt 1lb.** ***Traverse:*** **4° left and right.** ***Range:*** **10,300 yards.** ***Rate of fire:*** **2 rounds per minute.** ***Height:*** **6 feet.** ***Width:*** **6 feet 6 inches.** ***Length:*** **21 feet 7 inches**

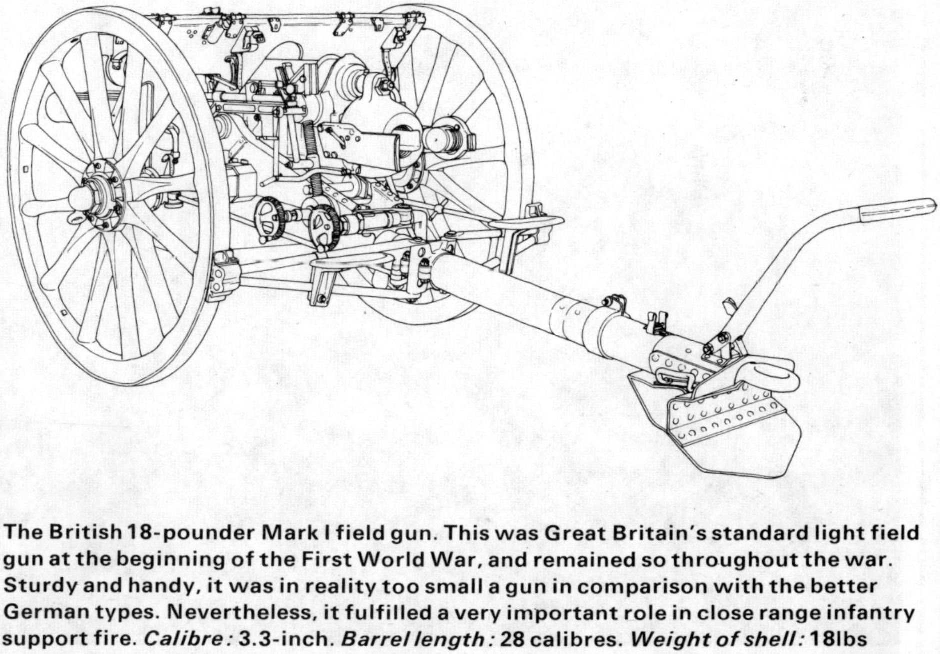

The British 18-pounder Mark I field gun. This was Great Britain's standard light field gun at the beginning of the First World War, and remained so throughout the war. Sturdy and handy, it was in reality too small a gun in comparison with the better German types. Nevertheless, it fulfilled a very important role in close range infantry support fire. ***Calibre:*** **3.3-inch.** ***Barrel length:*** **28 calibres.** ***Weight of shell:*** **18lbs** ***Range:*** **7,000 yards.** ***Elevation:*** **—5° to +16°.** ***Weight of gun and carriage:*** **3,800lbs**

battery fire, to smother German retribution against British guns and infantry forming-up places. And the rôle of the real prima donnas, the gigantic 12- and 15-inch howitzers, was the engagement of long-range targets, such as the key village of Monchy le Preux with its complex of command and control installations and the railway sidings at Biache St Vaast. Still further afield would be added the aerial bombing of Douai and other such places whenever the atrocious weather permitted flying and the bombers could fight their way past superior German fighter formations.

The standard of British gunnery was higher at Arras than it had been on the Somme. The integration of more efficient meteorology made shooting more accurate (the day when a battery commander decided the standard correction for the day by the drift of smoke from his first cigar was passing), while measures were introduced to give observers adequate opportunities to detect and correct the fall of shot. Fuses still gave trouble, however. The 18-pounder lacked a good, instantaneous fuse while another type was all too instantaneous for its friends, as a Canadian gunner tells us: 'We were in front of seven lines of guns and there were six batteries behind firing prematures at us. All day and all night the air above was filled with the whine of shrapnel bullets from premature bursts and the howl of fuses and shell cases. The only real protection we built in that position was in the form of thick sand-bag walls behind the guns to keep out our own shrapnel.'

A great upheaval by high explosives would pulverise the countryside with ponderous monstrosity up to the morning of the assault. Then a totally new method would come into play – the establishment of creeping, linear barrages behind which the infantry would endeavour to advance. The isolation of each successive objective by

The week of suffering. The Germans under bombardment on Vimy Ridge

Bombing aircraft – small complement to the night artillery

standing barrages was designed to prevent the intervention of German reserves, the systematic soaking of enemy gun-positions with gas to hamper the gunners and kill the horses that pulled the guns or resupplied ammunition. But none of this would happen until two weeks or more of steady downpour from thousands of shells had told the Germans the extent of the area most threatened. Loss of surprise was inevitable after a barrage of such dimensions had lasted for more than forty-eight hours. Yet surprise gained from the sheer weight of an assault and maintained in momentum by excellent organisation might just throw the defenders off balance. But how much more could be achieved if the assault were delivered at an unexpected time – earlier, for instance, than previous experience led the Germans to believe it would come?

On Vimy Ridge, where sheer brute force was to be the Canadian Corps' keynote, surprise was at a discount, but General Allenby, commanding Third Army, was more subtle – or tried to be. Of all the British army commanders he was the most receptive to new ideas and most anxious to restore the vital element of surprise to the battlefield. In Major-General A E Holland, his MGRA, he possessed a highly imaginative collaborator who, in thought and boldness, was somewhat ahead of Birch at GHQ. Holland proposed to compress the entire preparatory bombardment into two days instead of the five prescribed by GHQ. He intended to intensify the rate of fire, yet to conserve gunners and guns by firing in regulated shifts. In refutation of Birch's criticism (that over-heating and excessive barrel wear would result), he referred to successful practical tests carried out with an 18-pounder and a 6-inch howitzer. But Holland's method depended upon much firing being aimed largely off the map with observation of results inevitably reduced to the barest minimum. Thus its effects, particularly on the German wire, could neither be assured nor easily measured. However, Birch was on even firmer ground when he pointed out that much of the heavy artillery was newly arrived in France and entering action for the first time. Its training was therefore incomplete and its performance a questionable factor. There was an *impasse*, deftly resolved by the age-old expedient of kicking Holland upstairs to command a corps elsewhere and giving his post to Major-General R St C Lecky whose acquiescence to GHQ doctrine was assured. Looking ahead, it is perhaps worth mentioning that, in places at Arras, even the five day bombardment failed to clear the wire and that the last minute and fortuitous postponement of the attack, with the addition of an extra twenty-four hours shooting, was of great benefit to the British assault when it came.

The bombardment on Third Army's front, which began on April 4th, widened in German estimation the frontage they expected to be attacked, though confirming their original belief that the primary Allied offensive would be against Vimy Ridge. The prolonged nature of the bombardment, catching every attention, distracted German GHQ into thinking, even as late as 7th April, that the British appeared only to be aiming for the Heights of Vimy 'as a springboard for further attacks' and therefore it was not yet 'the great breakthrough offensive'. The staging of the bombardment thus became an important though unintended deception. As a factor of destruction, however, it was far less effective than had been hoped, falling as it did upon an opponent whose dispositions, north of the

German howitzer – silenced by a misconceived policy

Scarpe, were obsolete and, to the south, anything but complete. On 6th April Group Vimy with 297 guns (seventy batteries) available had lost only one battery destroyed: Group Arras, out of 352 guns, had lost but thirteen. Of course, as time went on, the scale of damage increased. But only in a few places, notably on the north wing of Group Arras by 8th April, was it serious. That the German artillery was in trouble and retaliating only in limited measure was, however, more the result of the German General Staff's miscalculations than the success of their enemy.

The British artillery had been denied full success from its counterbattery work by a combination of difficulties – the fact that, north of the Scarpe, the German guns lay tucked close under the lee of Vimy Ridge or in deep gulleys running parallel to the front and at right angles to the Scarpe itself. Observation from the air and the correction of accurate fire was made haphazard at a time when German aircraft destroyed great numbers of British observation aircraft thus interrupting concentration on their task. This period in the air was called 'Bloody April' with Richthofen and his men absolutely in command. It was significant that the British obtained their best counterbattery results only against those guns located in the more open ground west of Gavrelle, a success that might have been further reduced if the German gun positions had been deployed in depth instead of situated in easily recognisable straight lines.

Another important German miscalculation stemmed from abstention from strenuous counterbattery work of their own. No serious attempt was made by their air force to exploit aggressively its technical advantage over the Allied lines to seek and destroy Allied guns and supplies. Their artillery was denied air observa-

The great German 42 cm mortar, missing from the front when most required

The battle of ammunition supply. Pack horses and mules make for the gun pits

tion except from balloons which, for reasons of survival, had to deploy some thousands of yards from the front. Nevertheless, the German forward observation officers on the ground occupied many fine viewpoints and, despite frequent interruptions of their telephone cables to the guns, were well positioned to harry the British gunners. But even though Ludendorff called for 'more shooting', Falkenhausen's Sixth Army withheld its fire because it calculated on there being insufficient ammunition at the front and believed that, such as there was, particularly in gas shells, should be conserved until the British attack began. The fact that 'mountains of shells piled up in Douai' was irrelevant if they did not reach the front. In any case the German artillery in action was well below strength in heavy pieces, most of which were out of the line engaged in training and not expected to reach the front until 10th April at the earliest. For instance, the two formidable 42cm batteries, whose task was conceived as the means to block Arras as a communication and route centre, had barely reconnoitred their positions before the British attacked.

In point of fact the Germans had been deceived as to both the timing and direction of the British offensive, an error they compounded with faulty infantry dispositions. Only on 5th April was it admitted that a major offensive could be expected within days instead of weeks – a likelihood that turned to certainty when, on the 6th, enemy cavalry was reported close by Arras. This was a momentous day, indeed – one in which the war entered a new dimension. This day the USA declared war on Germany.

Throughout, however, an air of suffocating optimism permeated German HQs at all higher levels, the failure of the British artillery to destroy so many guns or to prevent the regular relief of units in the line attributing powerfully to this feeling. The fact that the rearward defence positions were incomplete and, in the case of the next main line of resistance, between Drocourt and Quéant, hardly begun, in no way ruffled the staffs' composure. Falkenhausen, basing his assumptions on the experience of the Somme, reckoned the forward divisions 'may perhaps lose sections of their front lines but cannot be overrun in their totality. It would suffice to move in the relief divisions on the evening of the second day of battle'. In practice this deployment of the reserve divisions made an early intervention impossible and even then it would only be as a relief and not for counterattack. Only 17th Division was within ten miles of the front, and therefore a day's marching away, and it was there purely as a labour force working on the rearward defences. None of the other four divisions in army reserve were closer than thirty miles distant, their extreme separation from the front the result of Falkenhausen's earnest desire to give them maximum rest along with vital training.

Rupprecht had ruled against this policy and wished all reserves to be within ten miles of the front before the British attack began, but his orders were disregarded or delayed – largely it seems through the inertia of Colonel von Nagel, Falkenhausen's Chief of Staff. By 10th April all might have been well, though it certainly was not on the 8th, when the attack was originally due to commence, nor even on the 9th when it actually started. For between the 6th and the 9th the German situation had visibly deteriorated as the British bombardment worked up to its climax.

By nightfall on the 8th conditions at the front were well nigh indescribable. Nearly everywhere the wire had been eliminated, the trenches blasted and filled to the level of the surrounding ground where shell craters intersected lip to lip. On the surface man could hardly move: below, those who survived existed in bemused terror, fixed between prayers for relief allied to a grim determination to remain under cover to the last possible moment. Those artillery observation posts which had missed being sucked into the whirlwind of destruction were isolated from their guns by the almost total severance of their telephone cables – even those which had been laid in triplicate and sometimes buried six feet deep. Here and there, but particularly on the Vimy Heights, the front line men were deprived of rations because a journey from the cookhouses which once took only fifteen minutes now lasted six hours in a rippled quagmire. Thus the food was both cold and fouled by mud before it arrived – as it often failed to do.

In conflicting states of calm, false optimism in their headquarters and abject terror and depression at the front, the Germans awaited their fate. Within the circumstances and the existent conditions of weapon development they had, in a manner of speaking, done everything possible to ease the Canadian and British task. It would remain to be seen if their opponents were capable of recognising – and capturing – the opportunity.

Easter Monday

The assault on the Heights of Vimy Ridge between Givenchy and the low ground by the River Scarpe followed three characteristically different procedures. Against the heights themselves, on the extreme left where the Germans were strongest of all, it was for 4th and 3rd Canadian Divisions to advance, two brigades abreast each with their third brigade in reserve, to the crest and there consolidate. Their frontage was narrow and the depth of their advance a mere 1,000 yards. 2nd Division, on 3rd Division's right, would have to advance twice that distance to its objective, however, and was therefore compelled to tackle the problem in two phases – two of its brigades taking the lead leaving two further brigades (its own plus the 13th British Brigade borrowed for the occasion) then to leapfrog and seize the lip of the ridge between Bois de Bonval and Farbus. Next in line to the right would come 1st Division attacking two brigades abreast, then pushing its third brigade through to the crest between Farbus and Bois de Farbus to constitute the right flank formation of Canadian Corps. Thus this reserve brigade would be the link between Canadian Corps in First Army and the left flank brigade of 51st Division in XVII Corps of Third Army.

The 51st Division filled the gap between the Canadians on the heights and the 34th and 9th Divisions which, as the battering ram for XVII Corps, were to prise open Third Army's main axis of advance north of the Scarpe. These three divisions opted, more or less, to attack with all three brigades in line abreast (though 51st had a variation of its own as befitted a Highland Division of strong individuality). There, however, any similarity with past techniques disappeared. Previously it had been the practice to maintain the momentum of an advance within the division by passing one brigade through another, but with the appearance of deep defensive systems this method proved insufficient to crack a front wide enough open to allow cavalry to enter undefended territory. Fresh and organised infantry were required to drive deeper in order to arrive in strength beyond the third German line – the line which ran from Méricourt to Fampoux on the Scarpe thence to link with the new Hindenburg Line near Wancourt south of the Scarpe. The 4th Division in XVII Corps therefore had the task of leapfrogging 9th Division and breaching this line by nightfall on the first day of battle.

Likewise, south of the Scarpe, VI Corps was to open a gap three divisions wide using, from left to right, 15th, 12th and 3rd Divisions, then passing through the second phase division – the 37th in this case – beyond the German third line in the direction of Monchy le Preux where it dominated the horizon to the east. Between the left flank at Givenchy and the right flank brigade of 3rd Division, where it entered the battle south of the Arras to Cambrai road, an extended wave of men was simultaneously to leave its trenches at 0530 hours – close behind the creeping barrage – and roll, ten divisions strong, in the wake of the flaming surf of shellfire eroding what was hoped to be an already broken German defensive system.

To the immediate right of VI Corps, VII Corps seemed to be consigned by Allenby to the function of a breakwater. This Corps, attacking with 14th, 56th, 30th and 21st Divisions in line with the intention of enlarging the breach to the south, was to be the first to test the Hindenburg Line proper. It was also to find itself at a distinct disadvantage from the outset, for here the line had receded from the originally prepared jumping off positions depriving the attackers of the shelter that might have been given by underground ways. Here, too, the Germans delayed backing into their new line to the last moment, preventing the British artillery from getting a good sight of the obstacles and then indulging in thorough destruction of the

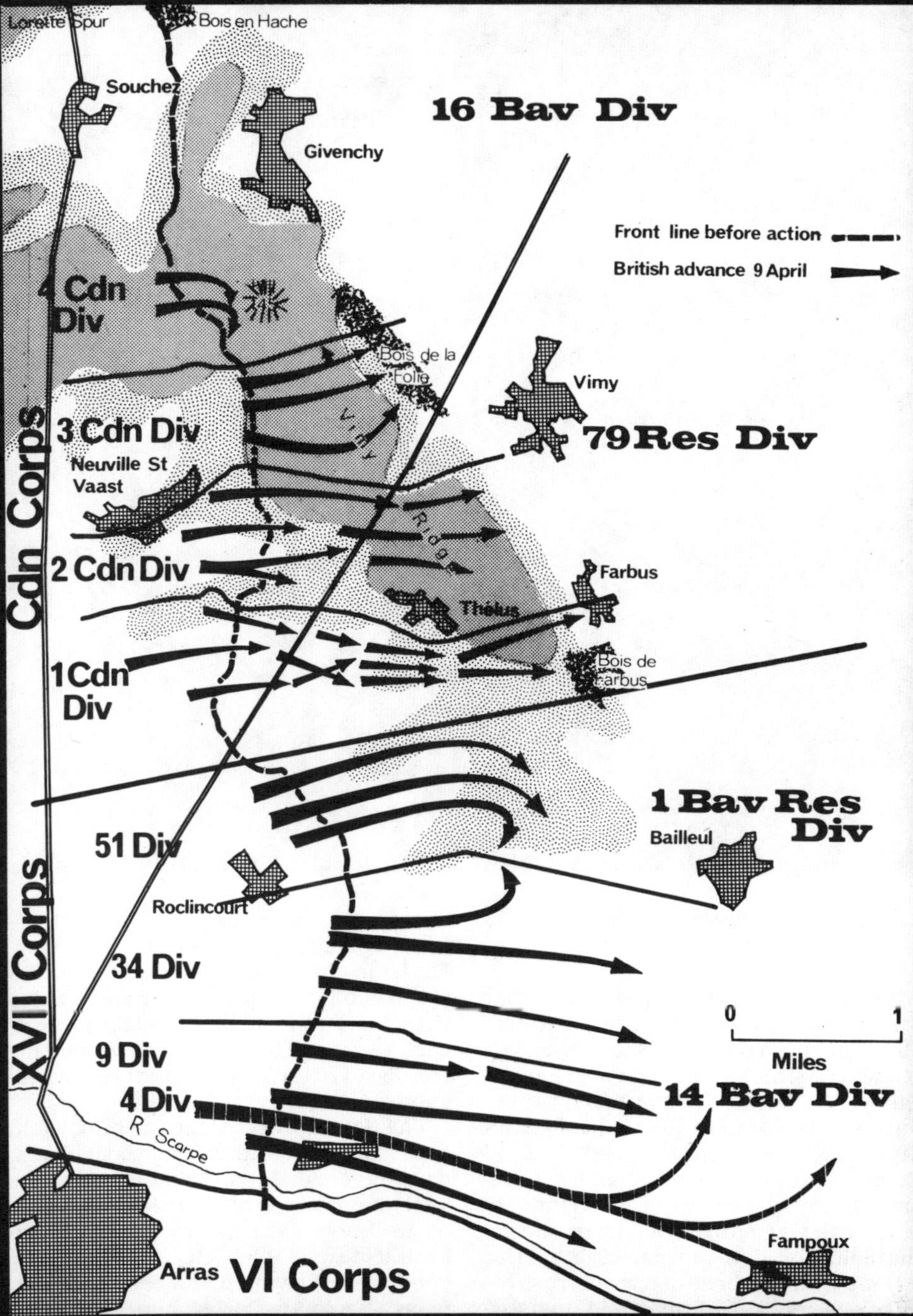

The Canadian and British advance on Vimy Ridge, Easter Monday, 9th April 1917

Canadian infantry wait for the assault

wire. And the wire here was truly formidable – deep and high banked, shining, as was said by those who saw it, 'with a sinister blue sheen'. General Snow, VII Corps Commander, wanted only to attack with his two left flank divisions, close to the right of VI Corps, leaving the erosion by penetration of these two formations to lever the Germans away from the remainder of his corps' front. But Allenby was determined to engross his entire Army's frontage and insisted upon every formation being engaged. So Snow, hoping to achieve a limited form of leverage, decided to attack in succession from the left – 14th Division starting two hours after 3rd Division until 21st Division finally stepped off as late as 1615 hours on the extreme right. Thus all surprise was cast away and each division stood the chance of attacking a well forewarned enemy.

The Cavalry Corps, meanwhile, with horses low in stamina due to the hard winter conditions, waited expectantly some eight miles from the front. As we know, 1st Cavalry Division had been retained by GHQ as a contingency reserve which had been omitted from Canadian Corps' plan. But 2nd and 3rd Cavalry Divisions were definitely to pass through the infantry south of the Scarpe once they reached a line

east of Monchy. Allenby, a cavalryman like Haig, was determined that this should be so. Nevertheless the cavalry were not expected to be through until late on the second day of the offensive, and thus they would tend to hang back on the first day, unavailable should a dramatic breakthrough be achieved at once.

Nothing so positive embraced French thinking or planning at this stage, however. Indeed Nivelle's ebullient schemes were crumbling before a shot had been fired, his basic concepts doubted by senior generals (most of whom had previously been senior to him) and some of the politicians. The German withdrawal disrupted and delayed French arrangements more than those of the British. Moreover, on 4th April a local German counterattack had penetrated the centre of the prospective zone of attack causing severe confusion and, worse, presenting the Germans with a written plan of the attack found on a French sergeant in the front line. Thereupon Nivelle had to concede the necessity on the 5th for a postponement by forty-eight hours – a respite which, as we have seen, was helpful to the British who merely retarded their attack by twenty-four hours to the 9th. But for the French there were yet more troubles in store followed by further delays. The date at last settled on the 16th, totally nullifying Nivelle's grand design for a simultaneous Allied attack with French predominance. But nothing could now stop Haig.

Before dawn on Easter Monday, 9th April, the guns drew breath after a night spent furiously battering German command posts and communication links. The previous day, a clear sunny but crisply chill Easter Sunday, had provided these gunners with the best shooting of the period, and the satisfaction of demolishing most of the German wire that remained. It was actually felt on both the Canadian and British sides that time spent studying some of Nivelle's methods from Verdun had been worthwhile.

Yet there was a discrepancy between those who attacked in the British army and those who were in Canadian Corps. The former had yet to compensate for the hideous losses of earlier years. Its standards of instruction and communication between officer and man left much to be desired – deficiencies which, in action on all too many occasions, led to breakdowns. Too often when an officer was killed there was simply nobody with the knowledge, experience or initiative to take up the torch. With the Canadians, on the other hand, there was a wholesale sharing of knowledge and confidence, as described by one of their officers prior to the Vimy

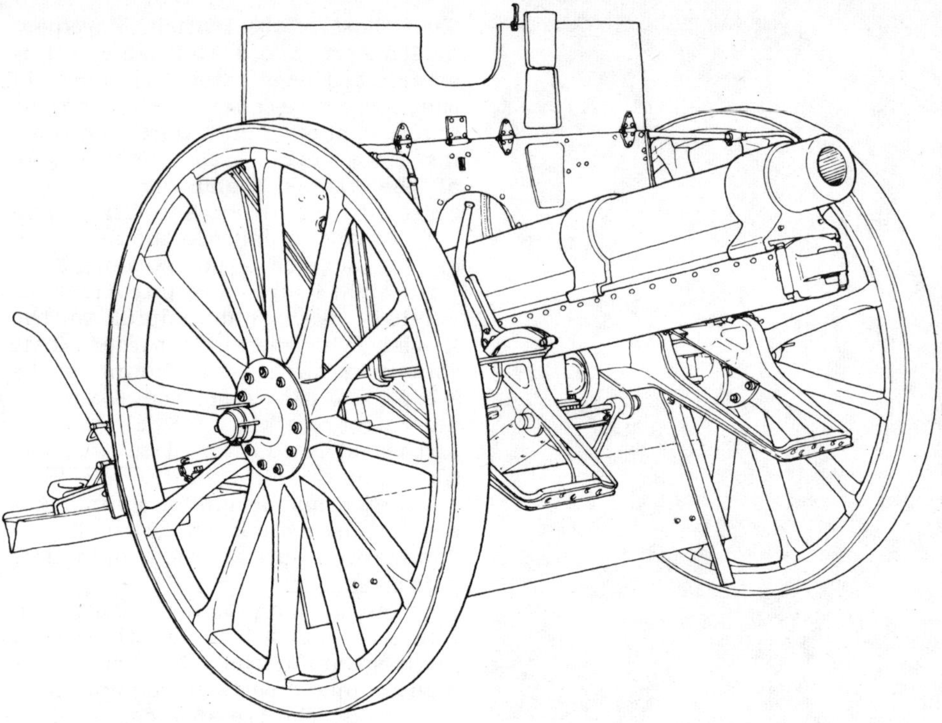

The German 7.7cm light field gun. ***Calibre:*** **7.7cm.** ***Barrel length:*** **23 calibres.** ***Weight of shell:*** **15lbs.** ***Elevation:*** **—13 to +15 .** ***Muzzle velocity:*** **1,523 feet per second.** ***Range:*** **9,200 yards.** ***Weight of gun in firing position:*** **2240lbs**

assault: 'We placed absolute trust in our men and took them entirely into our confidence. Instead of issuing a few maps to the officers, every single man was taken to see large-scale maps and a clay model reproduction of the battlefield and its objectives. We were confident that no one would desert and divulge information. And no one did.'

In the Canadian rearward areas there was a feeling of victory even before the attack had begun – '. . . the whole of the back country was filled with music: brass bands, bugle bands, pipe bands, fife and drum bands in the darkness were playing their units out to history.' Some marched to the forming up trenches under the cover and in the dry of the underground ways. Others struggled through the morass on the surface, past gun pits lit by the flash of each round on a night which got icily cold as it neared the dawn.

From both sides tension converged upon the front line trenches. For their part the Germans of 79th Reserve Division became aware of the Canadian trenches filling up to their front, the moonlight reflected on helmet tops, but the artillery fire so badly needed to crush the Canadians before they came further was wanting. Having conserved their ammunition for this very moment there was no way for the Germans to ask their gunners to fire because the observation parties were either dead or their telephone cables cut. Meanwhile the Canadian and British gunners were expectantly restocking and checking their ammunition for the climactic barrage due so soon to begin – each battery aligned to the strip of land over which its guns were to work, each No. 1 of a gun crew provided with a list of essential data – ranges and bearings – that would allow him to engage the exact area within the battery's strip and enable him to maintain accurate fire, lifting ahead 100 yards every five minutes. When zero hour came each battery commander would give the order to fire, relying on the No. 1s to supervise the rhythmic service of their guns by ammunition numbers and loader, the accurate pointing of the gun by the layer and exact compliance with the data laid down by Battery HQ. There was no room for error. To overshoot was to miss the target, to shoot short was to kill your own infantry. And, by the same counter, any attempt at interference with or modification of this meticulously calculated programme once it had started was to be resisted. Gunnery officers knew that to do so might cause No. 1s to make the very mistake the careful data list was designed to prevent.

Between Arras and the Lorette spur, at 0530 hours, the sky lit bright with the flash of many thousands of guns, the earth heaved and the air pulsated. Seconds later the German front line trenches, from Givenchy to Tillois, disappeared beneath a torrent of high explosive as, east of the Ridge, German gun crews became aware of soft thudding noises that announced the arrival of lethal gas shells to make their positions practically untenable. All round a nine mile arc the Canadian and British infantry, clambering out of their trenches, seemed to pause at the entrance to Hell. But it was a far more terrible moment for the Germans. Those caught on the surface might either be blown to pieces, buried or shot down by the fire of nearly 400 machineguns (on the Canadian front alone) laying a beaten zone of bullets across the crest line. In the pre-dawn gloom vision was, in any case, restricted, but sleet and snow, now driven by the wind, lashed their faces and made accurate shooting extremely difficult. To shift from place to place became a task in itself. For the wounded the likelihood of falling into some innundated trench or shell-hole, there to be drowned, was never remote. Some idea of the ground conditions can be obtained from the experience of a Canadian when he remarked: 'In one place I had to get out of my boots, climb on the bank of a sunken road and then pull my boots out after me'.

Into this sloppy quagmire 4th Canadian Infantry Division stumbled, keeping as close to the barrage as they dared. To their left a smoke screen obscured Bois en Hâche and the Pimple. Ahead stood the hump of Hill 145, battered, but not wholly devoid of defences. For the Germans had repaired some part of the damage and the Canadian infantry had declined an offer by their gunners to demolish them again because they thought to make use of the works themselves. Mostly 4th Division fell behind the barrage (hardly surprising when it is remembered they had to cross 250 yards of sticky No-Mans Land) to find themselves exposed to a determined enemy, emerging full of fight from the double fortified line on the hill-top and from deep underground works cut into the rearward slope – the so-called Hangstellung. Those of the attackers who passed to the north of the Hill mostly reached their objectives, there to explore the most remarkable underground dwellings they had ever seen; great caverns filled with every sort of supply from ammunition to cigars and Perrier water. Here was accommodation for between 250 and 300 men, and one such garrison was captured by the determination and bluff of a single Canadian officer, Captain MacDowell, assisted by a mere two men. Yet most who approached Hill 145 direct were stopped in their tracks so that, in consequence, those who passed to its south were enfiladed all day and prevented from taking all their objectives. Nevertheless those Canadians

Near Thélus; the dead, the ditched and the living

who actually reached the crest were not to be budged and the continued German resistance on Hill 145 was allowed to be no more than a local annoyance.

The setback on Hill 145 did nothing to deflect 3rd Division from its main purpose. Moving with fluent ease despite the mud, it kept close behind the barrage and swept among the Germans before they could climb to their parapets and come into action. Many Germans, in fact, were found in a state of undress. Others were pursued helter skelter along the communication trenches, into the shattered Bois de la Folie, with commanders and staffs subjected to the same rough handling as their men. It was from this part of the Ridge that the Canadians first truly appreciated the importance of seizing the crest. A Private Breckenridge recalls: 'In the valley before us we could see the Germans withdrawing their guns' . . . a sight all too rarely granted to infantry in this war.

Indeed these German guns had hardly fired a shot for the good reason that they were unaware of the position of friend and foe up on the ridge. In the gloom they did not notice the distress flares fired into the air by the hard pressed infantry. A German infantryman in 1st Bavarian Reserve Regiment, which bore the brunt of assault

by the Canadian right wing, expressed the feelings of the majority: 'In the north and south his [the enemy's] masses continuously flow past the rock that was once in the hands of Reserve Infantry Regiment 2. In the midst of this upsurge all hope of relief diminishes. Where is our artillery, where our reserves, where our aircraft? Nothing comes – nothing at all. Hoping, waiting, enduring the icy snow gusts quarter hour after quarter hour passes by'. In scattered groups men such as these fought back and took their toll, but from this moment, in fact, the German infantry began repeatedly to complain of 'feeling deserted by the artillery', a state of affairs which boded evil for the future.

To who else could they turn for help?

The leading brigades of 2nd and 1st Canadian Divisions were no less eager and successful than those of the 3rd. Nor did it matter that the eight tanks allocated soon bogged down in the morass. The infantry had no need for them, not even where scattered and bewildered German machinegunners raised local resistance. The Canadian infantry virtually took over ground captured in advance by their artillery, practising linear tactics when opposition was slight, but automatically reverting to the role of individual hunters with bomb and bayonet once a machinegun fired. Two Victoria Crosses were won in this manner – by men who, on their own initiative, outwitted the Germans in solo combat. Even when the fighting was thickest, however, the outward signs of order were preserved, the CO of 16th Battalion in 1st Division advancing with an escort of pipers followed by his RSM and a soldier carrying two jars of rum apiece under their arms. By 0715 hours both 2nd and 1st Divisions were secure on their first objectives, busy gathering a rich haul of prisoners and the 77mm field guns which had been dug into the more advanced positions as a defence against tanks. And already the orders for the next wave of brigades to advance had gone out and they were breasting the slope in wonderment at hundreds of disarmed Germans streaming past them under escort to the rear. Victory was in the air and the fortified village of Thélus, overhanging the crest, beckoned.

From the air a somewhat detached, though no less exciting, view could be had of the battle. Captain Billy Bishop, a Canadian who was to become a legend to his countrymen, was flying 'contact patrols' that morning – that is skimming between low clouds and the ground to search for and then report the progress of the leading infantry who, upon the sound of a klaxon horn blown by the aircraft, were meant to mark their position by flares. This was dangerous work for the pilots. Apart from the risk of destruction by enemy small arms fire there was always the possibility of being struck by shells from the barrage. Bishop has written, 'The ground seemed to be one mass of bursting shells . . . Over and over again one felt a sudden jerk under the wing tip and the machine would heave quickly. This meant a shell had passed within a few feet of you . . . The waves of attacking infantry as they came out of their trenches and trudged forward behind the curtain of shells . . . were an amazing sight. The men seemed to wander across No-Mans' Land and into the enemy trenches as if the battle was a great bore to them. From the air it looked as though they did not realise that they were at war and were taking it all too quietly.' And in a manner of speaking that was nearer the truth, in some respects, than Bishop can have guessed.

Even as the leading brigades of 2nd and 1st Divisions arrived on the intermediate objective a total breakthrough was recognisable – but with nothing nearby to exploit it. Neither Horne's First Army nor Byng's Canadian Corps had planned in detail for this possibility, despite Haig's original desire that they should. On the other hand GHQ had earlier cancelled the order placing 1st Cavalry Division under Horne leaving this division at rest some distance from the front. But now, close to his troops at the front, Major-General Arthur Currie, commanding 1st Canadian Infantry Division, was pressing hard for the leading brigades to continue the advance to the crest without waiting for the follow up brigades. It was all too obvious in his sector that German resistance had utterly collapsed and, indeed, a German was to record that, 'Nothing was known of the situation of the infantry on the ridge, since all telephone cables leading forward . . . had been broken and patrols sent forward could bring no enlightenment.'

Captain Bishop

German guns lay close under the ridge but had practically ceased firing for want of an identifiable target. If the Canadians had gone on marching they would have reached the crest by 0800 hours.

As it was the British artillery intervened – correctly by the book but in precisely the wrong way for the circumstances. The next phase of the barrage was not due to lift forward until 0935 hours and the gunners insisted that to tamper with the programme would be hazardous. So everybody paused for more than two hours, waiting to advance into a vacuum while the artillery indulged in what is sometimes now called an 'overkill'. Thus the British and Canadian brigades in 2nd Division and the reserve brigade in 1st Division were prevented from reaching the crest until 1300 hours. When they got there, of course, there lay revealed a spectacle which fascinated – almost overwhelmed – Canadian emotions, a view to be described over and over again in histories and personal memoirs – the sight of the waiting plain beyond, populated by isolated and scurrying Germans, and the realisation that the numerous enemy guns, lying exposed to view, were theirs to capture from a quick charge to the bottom of the slope.

The existence of surviving and desperate German defenders who killed so many Canadians at the moment of triumph could almost be overlooked in so complete a victory. For the Germans, too, this was a moment of

mystique as recounted in their official post-war monograph, *Die Osterschlacht bei Arras:* 'The cessation of the snowstorm lifted the veil which had till now hidden the landscape and we saw a remarkable sight. The air was suddenly clean and clear, filled with spring sunshine. The high ground about Thélus was covered with English (sic) storm troops standing about in large groups . . . For a few moments the artillery fire almost ceased on both sides and complete silence fell upon the battlefield, as if all were lost in wonder. The battle itself seemed to hold its breath.'

Apart from the exceptions imposed by the bitter fighting, still going on around Hill 145, and in the chase to the bottom of the slope, that particular

'Storm troops standing about in large groups'

German judgement was appropriate. The battle did hold its breath as both Canadians and Germans tried to pump more life into it. Belatedly Byng was endeavouring to push cavalry forward to exploit what was all too evidently a wholesale enemy collapse. The Germans were striving to fill the yawning gap with what few men they could scrape up from units not already committed to the line. But 1st Cavalry Division was out of reach and the only Canadian horsemen to cross the crest and enter the Plain of Douai on the afternoon of the 9th comprised a squadron divided into two small patrols which advanced unopposed to the village of Willerval until they were ejected by German artillery and machinegun fire. This the Germans interpreted as a large cavalry force repelled as, about the same time, their own reserves also began to appear – three battalions rushed down from Lille and thrown precipitately into the line with somewhat vague orders to counterattack. They succeeded, in the end, merely in filling gaps in the line as they came under fire from the Canadian artillery whose observers had now established communication with the guns from the crest.

It would be some time before the Canadian guns could be dragged forward to extend their reach to the east since the state of the ground utterly forbade movement. And it would be many hours, if not days, before roads could be relaid through the morass caused by months of shelling. Moreover, engineering work on the Canadian right was somewhat delayed because 51st Division had failed to take all its objectives and was hanging back.

51st Highland Division's troubles are easily stated. The divisional commander, a bigoted man called Harper, had rejected the reasoned proposals of his superiors in favour of a system of his own making for the assault. He had tampered with the organisation of his brigades in order to create a small divisional reserve for himself and overloaded the capacity of the two brigades that remained committed to the assault on a broad front. Things had gone wrong from the outset as units, driven to work under unfamiliar headquarters, lost direction in the assault and finished up in a communication trench they swore blind was the objective. Thus they were at right angles to the axis of attack and had opened a gap between the Canadians and themselves, thereby stalling the remainder of 51st Division's advance and exposing the left flank of

Two small horsed patrols make for Willerval

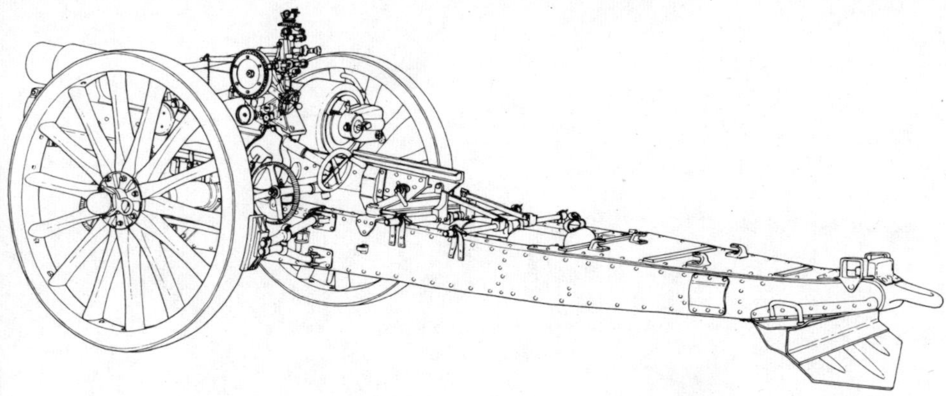

The British 6-inch howitzer Mk I. *Calibre:* 6-inch. *Weight of shell:* 100lbs. *Elevation:* 0 to +45 . *Traverse:* 8 . *Range:* 10,000 yards. *Weight of gun and carriage:* 72cwt 2qtrs 22lbs

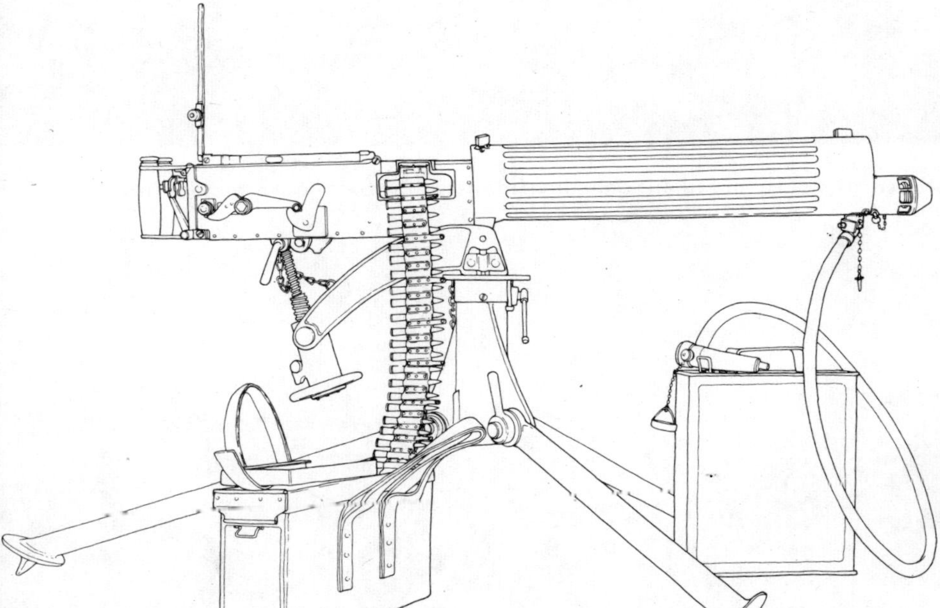

The Vickers .303-inch Machine Gun Mark 1 was the standard machine gun in use by British forces in both world wars, and was a sturdy (if heavy) and reliable weapon. It is shown mounted on a Mark IVB tripod. *Calibre:* .303-inch. *Method of operation:* Recoil with gas boost from a muzzle booster. *Weight of gun:* 33lbs (without water). *Weight of tripod:* 50lbs. *Coolant:* Water (7lbs in weight). *Length:* 43 inches. *Barrel length:* 28.4 inches. *Ammunition supply:* Canvas belts, each holding 250 rounds. *Muzzle velocity:* 2,440 feet per second. *Cyclic rate of fire:* 450-550 rounds per minute

Above: The old game again: Canadian infantry dig in on the crest under fire

Below: **The guns dig in behind them**

Canadian artillerymen turn a German gun against its previous masters

34th Division, next in line to the south. In consequence 34th Division had to dissipate some of its effort in flinging back a flank guard instead of advancing full strength to the crest overlooking Bailleul. What was worse, nobody – not even Currie, who was well forward and perfectly aware of what had gone wrong – could convince Harper of the error of his men since Harper, with insufferable obstinacy, was not one to admit to a failure by 51st Division. Fortunately the Tyneside infantry in 34th Division could put right by sheer fighting ability what the Highlanders' General had spoilt by misplaced pride. In fact, throughout the altercation, the way lay almost clear to the crest. First Bavarian Reserve Division had all but disintegrated under the gunfire. Only a few of its scattered machinegun posts barred the way and these were soon despatched by the Tynesiders – albeit at a price.

This departure of defenders from the Ridge, from opposite Bailleul past the Point de Jour down to the Scarpe, was, when allied to the neglible volume of German gunfire, one of the most remarkable features of an astonishing day. For a few hours even the German higher command deluded itself that the Ridge remained securely held along its length, totally unaware, as they were, of the magnitude of the catastrophe. Indeed those of the British who advanced on the right of 34th suffered the traumatic experience first, of desperate fighting against Germans in front line trenches, (whose occupants had fought with the determination of old), then of a headlong, unopposed rush to the Ridge Line. Ninth Scottish Division, three brigades abreast – two of Scotsmen and one of South Africans – cleared the trench network north of St Laurent and entered a vacuum. The four tanks allotted to them bogged in the mud, but fundamentally it was a desperate race to keep up with the barrage, provided by twelve Heavy Groups, and reach the Ridge before German morale became re-established.

In exhilaration – the scene and atmosphere caught by an officer who was there – the 9th exchanged their fear of the horrors of trench fighting for the apprehensions of open warfare.

'Even the pill-boxes seemed to show no sign of life. What could it mean? Some trap no doubt and we set our teeth and went for the wire. It was a tough job getting through the wire, even with little or no opposition, and then we saw an inspiring sight – a mob of Boche hareing out of the trenches. It was too much for the Borderers who raced us to the Point du Jour. What a sight it was when we got there! One could see half the world, and everywhere one looked were fleeing Boches. Even far away Monchy seemed covered with fugitives.

'The telephone spoke to Frank Maxwell [27th Brigade's dashing commander]: "Are the Boches on the run? Is cavalry good business?"

"Yes, ten thousand times yes, but it must be done now. Too late tomorrow. Why can't we go on? . . ." '

Why not indeed? But the original plan was not to be changed. The nearest cavalry were six miles off to the west and between stood 4th Division still awaiting permission to march to the gap. The cries of success from units of 9th Division had to wend their way back through brigade to division and then to corps HQ before they could be translated into orders and relayed to 4th Division. Had XVII Corps commander (General Fergusson) been at the front to see the situation for himself he might have short-circuited the whole business – even allowing 9th Division to go on. Perhaps even to cancel the barrage.

A German gun which did not escape

Proof of success: Canada's prisoners pour in

But Fergusson waited, perforce, at the centre of a communication web, sifting the evidence of others and making his decisions by *coup de telephone* instead of *coup d'oeil*. Fourth Division did not set off from Arras until 1000 hours, two hours after 9th Division reached the Point du Jour, and did not go into the lead behind the barrage until 1500 hours. By then daylight was wearing short and soon, in any case, the barrage was in decline as many guns ceased fire at maximum range. Nevertheless, as night began to fall, the leading infantry entered Fampoux against only scattered opposition, though coming under persistently heavier fire from the railway embankment beyond. Yet Fourth Division had broken through as thoroughly as had the Canadians up on the heights, and in so doing had recorded an advance of three and a half miles – the longest achieved since trench warfare had begun. How much more

it might have been had they been allowed to start sooner, how much swifter had cavalry been in their place instead of trotting through Arras, two bounds behind at that moment, was a matter for conjecture.

Indeed as evening arrived the way was clear for the British to move almost unimpeded across the length of Vimy Ridge. A yawning gap almost five miles wide split the German defences and they could only send scattered groups to close it. Most of their forward artillery had been lost and that which arrived to take its place could only improvise. But this was not all. South of the Scarpe equally dramatic events were taking place and the entire German front lay in jeopardy. Well might Rupprecht write in his diary, 'Now we have to suffer because the Sixth Army, despite my strongest wishes, failed to ... move its reserves closer to the front-line divisions'. He might have reflected, too, on a staff system which prevented him from imposing his personal will, as commander.

Towards Cambrai

While it would be wrong to claim that the Canadian triumph on the Vimy Heights started the rot which crumbled the entire German position on the Ridge as far down as the Scarpe, it is undeniable that the awe-inspiring sequence of events in the north influenced German reaction elsewhere to an unwonted degree. Every German account gives precedence to events on the northern flank since it was there that the threat seemed greatest and in that direction that the greater proportion of reinforcements were despatched. Yet, as we know, the intended centre of gravity of Allenby's attack was actually south of the Scarpe, its centre line the Arras/Cambrai road, its objectives for the first day a line running east of Monchy. Lieutenant General Haldane's VI Corps was to achieve a profounder concentration in time and space than anywhere else – three divisions attacking on a 900-yard front, each with two brigades up and their third close behind for the follow-through: these to be leapfrogged by another fresh division – the 37th – whose task it was to take Monchy. All enjoyed the shelter of tunnels in their walk from the centre of Arras to the front. On this front no less than nine Heavy Artillery Groups were to play. Of tanks there were to be some twenty available (partly shared with VII Corps on the right) but unfortunately six fell into a deep bog on the way to the front and were thus missing from the attack on Tillois. Even so the weight of metal in support of men was immense – as the battered state of German 11th Division to their front bore testimony.

Nevertheless, as all three divisions struck out at 0530 hours on 9th April, they at once became heavily embroiled in the German forward trenches which, north of the main road, conformed in layout to the outmoded system of a preponderance of men at the front with far fewer held in safety behind. Each British division had as its principal objective, however, something more material than a mere line of trenches: they aimed directly for those interlocked topographical features which dominated the surrounding countryside. In the case of 15th Scottish Division, advancing nearest the river, their objective of most importance was a great railway embankment rearing high at the junction of three tracks (called Railway Triangle) its sides honeycombed with weapon pits whose machineguns could sweep and dominate both sides of the river. One of its leading brigades, from the outset, ran into fierce street fighting on the outskirts of Blangy while the other, which moved cross-country, was hacked down by fire from the Triangle. Yet strangely enough the Germans seemed unaware of the adverse effects they were causing, for they expressed surprise that the British did not advance any faster than they did. In fact, so hung up were his men that, eventually General McCracken, 15th Division's commander, felt compelled to overrule his gunners' objections and give a second dose of the barrage to the Triangle. Yet the final resolution of the German resistance in the Triangle came from another source, as described by the Germans themselves:

'Suddenly . . . a dark monster detaches itself from the ruins . . . and

The bands play in Arras Grande Place before the battle. The tunnels run below

slowly, very slowly, creeps along the road . . . towards the railway; not faster, not slower, as if each metre of its crawling advance depended on some other movement. Not faster, not slower than the pace of a man who has to force his every step through a thicket of obstacles. Convulsive bursts flash from its sponsons and little impact clouds are dancing along the ground to the same rhythm, accompanied by the short, sharp hammering of a machine gun whose shots hiss across the railway into the hinterland.' This was the tank *Lusitania*, slow at its best pace but here made slower still by the constant need to stop to cool an overheating engine. Its effect on Railway Triangle, however, was decisive, though it was not until 1230 hours that the fortress had fallen and both brigades could finally take their objectives.

Likewise there had been stiff fighting for both 12th and 3rd Divisions in the vicinity of Tillois. The former went over the top quite unscathed from German artillery fire – partly as the result of an artillery smoke screen laid across a rounded feature known as Observation Ridge which, stretching north from Tillois, provided shelter and viewpoints for the German observers and a breastwork for the mass of their guns lying in Battery Valley on the farther side. German resistance in these parts was uneven: some fought to the death and caused heavy losses, but others capitulated at once and surrendered from their dugouts. Everywhere it was the heroism of individual defenders who held up the advance, or attackers who destroyed key machine guns. The greater mass of infantry merely played walk-on parts, giving moral but somewhat mute support to the leading and bravest soloists. Each side had its problems – the German defenders were shaken to the core by the barrage, felt deserted by their gunners (who indubitably played little part) and had to fire into the teeth of the snow

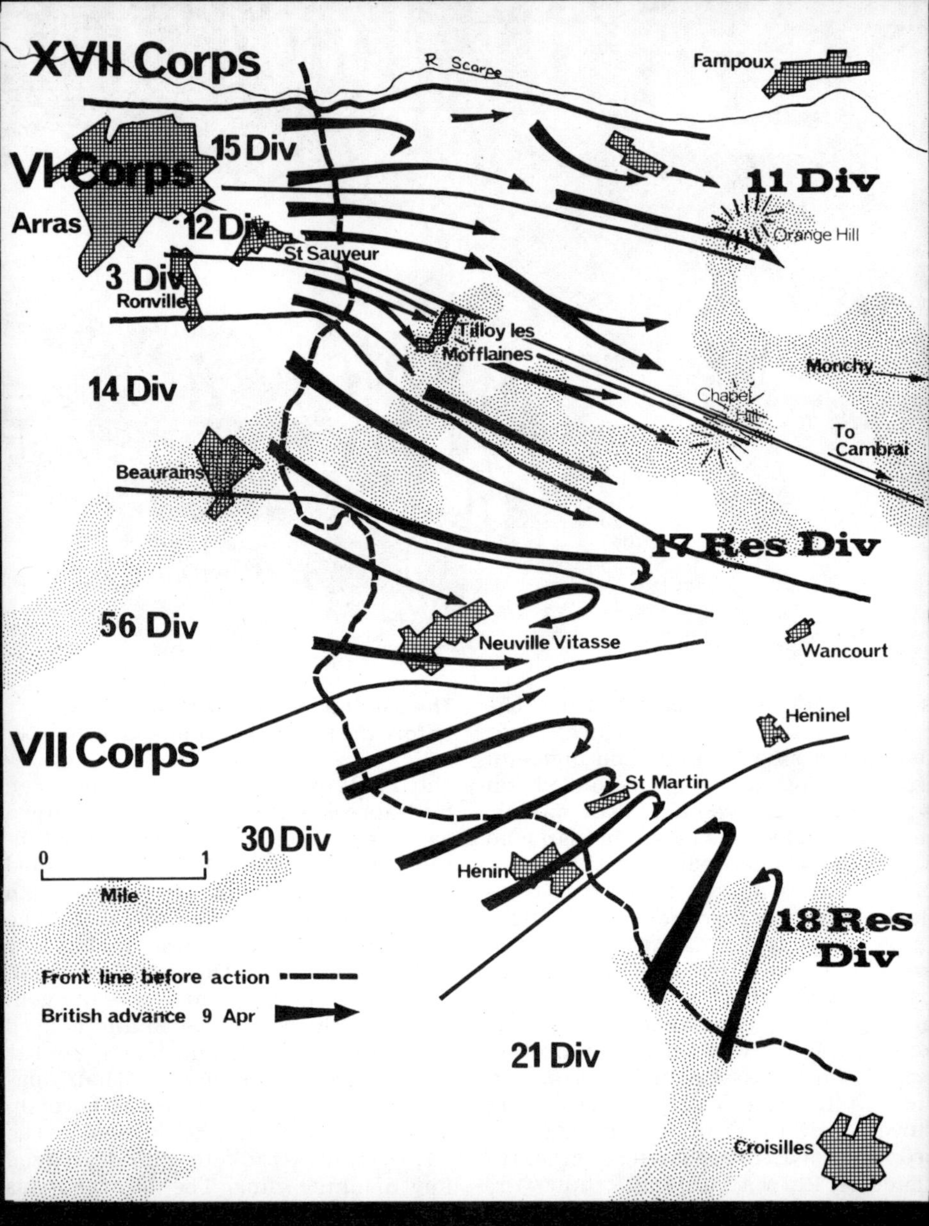

The British advance south of the River Scarpe, 9th April 1917

Above: Over the top. *Below:* Lusitania advances to decide the battle

German infantryman, 1917. Still wearing the *feldgrau* uniform of 1914, the German infantryman's pristine smartness had been allowed to decline under the exigencies and demands of trench warfare. Note that all German front line troops had by this date been issued with the 'coal-scuttle helmet', which can be distinguished from its Second World War counterpart by the depth of the skirt at the back and the twin protuberances at the side, the latter left by the manufacturing process. The soldier in the illustration is carrying the Gewehr 98a carbine, favoured over the basic rifle by many for its shorter length, and consequent handiness. In his left hand he is carrying an ammunition box, while there can also be seen the handle of his entrenching tool protruding from behind his back, the canisters for his gas mask and mess tools, and satchels for sundry equipment such as grenades

storm as the British closed in upon them. The British attackers, fearful of a repetition of the Somme with the scythe of small-arms fire cutting them down in swathes, were mainly held back by the sheer weight of equipment hanging about them. Each started with some 170 rounds of ammunition and two Mills grenades plus a mass of other accoutrements. Some wore jerkins and some great-coats; all were festooned with packs, water bottles and entrenching tools. Unhappily a man carrying half his own weight in equipment (that got heavier as water drenched it) can hardly move with agility let alone fight and take evasive action against an entrenched opponent. So it was hardly surprising that the path of many units could be traced not only by their dead but also by a trail of divested apparel.

At Tillois there was initial resistance to 3rd Division and a stiff fight for one trench in particular, but as fresh British infantry appeared, the ground sprouted Germans running into the open with their hands held high. This was a repetition of events

Canadian private, 1917. The Canadians wore the basic British uniform. Noteworthy here are the cap-comforter, which would be replaced by the helmet in action, and the leather jerkin, first issued in the winter of 1914. Much else of his equipment is standard, such as the SMLE rifle, entrenching tools and cut-down pack containing such essentials as mess tools but no greatcoat. He carries, like his German counterpart, satchels for extras such as grenades, extra ammunition and the like

on the Somme in that offensive's closing days – cause for British optimism and acute German dissatisfaction – the very signs of decay in the German army which Ludendorff and his entourage most feared.

Throughout the afternoon the onward rush continued as each division threw in its reserve brigade and 37th Division began its march through Arras (quite unhindered by enemy artillery fire which left the city strangely undisturbed), directed upon Monchy. Excitement mounted as the German second line came into sight. Forty-sixth Brigade in 15th Division, partially delayed by events at Railway Triangle, was left unaware of McCracken's decision to repeat the barrage on their front. Thus their leading battalion found itself out in the open in the awful predicament of having to wait for 'friendly' guns to play across them as the barrage of shells crept forward, for a second time, towards Observation Ridge. Cringing in whatever cover they could find, this battalion of Highland Light Infantry escaped miraculously with very few casualties, and then leapt to their feet on the fringes of the gunfire to charge the crest, before debouching among rows of German guns left abandoned beyond. Now it could be seen that, even if Battery Valley was ideal in terms of protection against fire for its occupants, it was also a death trap because it was *too* close to the front. Already, 12th Division had reached the crest and charged, blasted at point blank range by a desperate enemy, but hotbloodedly running down the slope to kill the German gunners at their posts. The Germans managed to put some guns out of action before abandoning them, but most they left behind, and in next to no time those British artillery officers who were marching with the infantry had formed scratch crews and taught them to fire the captured pieces in the general direction of their previous owners.

In exultation and triumph, however, lay the seeds of delay. Each setback and each skirmish distracted the infantry and left them farther behind the artillery schedule. Yet neither on 3rd nor 12th Divisions' fronts would the gunners adjust the barrage in sympathy. Inexorably it crept away from the men it was meant to help, so that at last, as 3rd and 12th Divisions marched out of Battery Valley to tramp through mud and slush towards the next tactical bound – the Feuchy Chapel and Orange Hill features – they became targets for untrammelled machine guns fired by those very few Germans who had not decamped, tardily reinforced by those who had fled and who had been caught by their officers and sent back. Yet really the sole and crucial problem for the British on Chapel Hill was wire – wire they could easily have cut by hand had the British artillery barrage been aimed upon Chapel Hill, neutralising its defenders, instead of rolling uselessly ahead into disengaged territory. The accumulative effects of each digression now took toll of 37th Division. Its two leading brigades – 111th and 112th – were detailed, respectively, to follow 12th and 15th Divisions. Both now became pinned by fire from Chapel Hill and thereby committed to the sort of brawl they had to avoid if they were to take Monchy by nightfall. Their one hope lay with 63rd Brigade Royal Field Artillery, following in rear and given the task of giving direct close support from Battery Valley. But seeing the infantry predicament at Chapel Hill the Brigade Commander brought his guns prematurely into action – though even then too late. For by then the infantry had been driven to ground. Once that has happened it usually takes hours to start them again, Chapel Hill was no exception to the rule.

Yet for all the obvious difficulties and minor setbacks a gaping hole lay open twixt Orange Hill and the river, a hole defiladed from Chapel Hill but only slightly defended. Into this vacuum strode 15th Division's 46th Brigade, envigorated by its success in Battery Valley and spearheaded by a most determined and fortunate tank which led the way down the length of the so-called Monchy Line, helping to destroy two machine guns and capturing 500 prisoners. Had 111th Brigade from 37th Division not drifted into 12th Division's sector, and become involved in 112th Brigade's private fight, it might now have broken through, unresisted, to Monchy. Even as it was McCracken reckoned 46th Brigade possessed the strength and will to go it alone, but he was refused permission by Haldane to do so and the task was given to 63rd Brigade, the remaining uncommitted element of 37th Division. But 63rd Brigade did not reach Battery Valley until 1800 hours, was without positive orders until 1935 and hardly breasting the slope of Orange Hill as darkness fell. And then everybody shut up shop, even though there was practically nothing to prevent them strolling unchecked into Monchy. Few were prepared to take risks at a time when quick daring might well have saved prolonged fighting. Indeed the 15th Division's cavalry regiment had actually slipped along the river flank to join hands with 4th Division at Fampoux – such was the open nature of the front at that moment. Cavalry, therefore, *were* good business and had been everywhere between Fampoux and Monchy since early that afternoon. The main body of the Cavalry Corps,

however, had yet to reach Arras for the simple reason that they were not expected to be needed until next day. So fast and complete had been the breakthrough south of Arras that, as in the north on Vimy Ridge, the pace of events had outrun the planners' preconceptions while, in matters of improvisation, leadership took second place to formality.

Not unexpectedly, the primary success by 14th Division where, as flank companion to the south of VI Corps it had attacked in echelon, had been disappointing. In VII Corps' sector each successive divisional attack, spaced out in time throughout the day from left to right, met stiffer and stiffer resistance in the toughest section of the Hindenburg Line proper against a forewarned opponent. General Snow's worst predictions were fully confirmed as 56th Division became caught in the fiercest and most unremitting close combat in Neuville Vitasse. Then 30th Division, coming later into action on its right against an unshaken enemy, failed to penetrate the German front line at all. Thus the attack by 21st Division on the right of the 30th towards the end of the afternoon became formal suicide – *hari kiri* of the most blatant kind. Here in deepest wire, quite uncut by a bombardment which had been the least well prepared and the most under-observed of any in Third Army, machineguns played the sort of havoc which had stamped its mark on every battle throughout 1915 and 1916. But with one vital difference. Here the new German system of defence was working efficiently, their guns taking a toll, their front line infantry largely saved from the holocaust, their local reserves moving smoothly and undetected into position for counter-attacks should the British break through. Theirs was the one bright spot in a day of black disaster for the Germans.

On the objective. The dead have been thrown over the parapet

Indeed almost everywhere German reactions stayed unduly calm as they assessed the state at the front on the evening of the 9th. It did not dawn upon them how severe had been their losses or complete the collapse of some formations. Falkenhausen would not even admit Vimy Ridge had fallen and, without precipitate haste, continued to feed minimum reserves towards the threatened areas – notably towards the Vimy Heights which fascinated his attention – as if nothing had happened at all. It was some time before he or Rupprecht would admit to a breakthrough having taken place and so the sealing off of the front was delayed still longer – to the benefit of the British for their easier exploitation. German losses – never easy to assess – had been immense; some 4,000 in 79th Reserve Division, 3,000 in 1st Bavarian Reserve, 4,000 in 14th Bavarian, 3,000 in 11th and 2,700 in 17th Reserve; while in guns they had lost fifty-four to the Canadians and a further sixty-seven in Battery Valley alone. Likewise the debilitated condition of the men seems only slowly to have come to the notice of their senior commanders. Some of them, like Falkenhausen, declined to withdraw to a safer line but, instead 'demanded Artillery reinforcements for systematic attack' – a request denied by Rupprecht for reason of the danger of attacking at the same time as the enemy. Attack, in fact, was quite beyond the capacity of the troops at the front. A junior officer in 79th Reserve Division, subsisting in peril at Vimy, wrote: 'The physical condition of the men is such that even the slightest exertion, such as doing guard duty, can only be endured by a few with any degree of certainty. We are deluding ourselves if we think we can make greater demands on the efficiency of the men . . . it is the lack of food which is undermining the men and, in particular, having to live in the open which has exhausted their resistance. Some people have already collapsed with fatigue and frost. Everyone is suffering constantly from shivering with cold.' Concomitant with this came the recognition by one German, General Diefenbach, that the combat had 'taken on the character of a mobile battle'.

The elements of mobile warfare were certainly present. British infantry roamed at large instead of burrowing narrowly below ground; cavalry wended its regal way towards the battle smoke with a clear cut prospect of getting into action; the guns began to pick up their trails, hook onto limbers and horses or tractors and start the laborious haul forward into conquered territory. And then the deficiencies which had been revealed in the pursuit of the Germans to the Hindenburg Line intervened. The system of quickly communicating orders to inexperienced men in a fast changing situation broke down almost everywhere – as it had, for instance, in 37th Division. Commanders at all levels tended to hang back – in the case of the highest because, in trench warfare, it was thought best to be at a communication centre in rear since little enough could be seen at the front: in the case of battalion commanders because they were *ordered* to follow and not lead their men in order to reduce the wholesale slaughter of experienced officers. Thus ill-trained men at the front were found lacking in direction and initiative and often missed seizing opportunities even when – so rarely – they recognised them. There was no way of hastening the arrival of the cavalry and no question of pushing them through during the night into unknown country. What was worse, they were averse to spending a night without fodder. They could have camped close behind the front – near Thélus on the Heights, behind Fampoux or in Battery Valley near the Scarpe. Instead they were withdrawn at dusk in order to be fed and watered at Arras. Thus they would take longer to reach the front next day and at dawn would be

Above: **Aftermath at Fampoux. The extent of artillery devastation is clear**
Below: **The second wave passes through**

unready to enter the gap which, on the 9th and 10th, lay wide open.

Few tanks survived to help and so, as usual, all depended upon the guns to blast German reinforcements as they appeared. By nightfall, however, the guns were mostly firing at extreme range and, in endeavouring to shift themselves forward, were entering the morass of their own making, the churned up ground east of Arras through which every road lay in ruins amid limpid fields. Tractor drawn heavies wallowed and sank. Horse-drawn field pieces struggled desperately as many of their teams died out of sheer exhaustion in the terrible conditions. One gunner tells how, 'We got them up somehow by relays, with twelve to fourteen horses in the guns and the gunners harnessed to the wagons'. Thus when pace was essential to maintain momentum behind a moving curtain of fire, ahead of the British infantry (whose losses were at that moment less than 12,000) and cavalry, there were abundant signs of a sharp rundown in the rate of advance – a rundown dictated by communication failures and inertia, compounded by sheer exhaustion.

Study in surprises

Although the Germans had been slow to recognise the imminence of an offensive and slower yet to gauge the cataclysmic effects of its onset, they were no less perceptive, in fact, than the British who, in their tardiness to seize the apple of victory dangling before them, let slip a peerless opportunity. When, throughout 9th April, the British and Canadians repeatedly eschewed improvisations to hasten the extension of their gains, it was a measure of their empirical scepticism and subservience to artillery procedures: but when they took refuge in a state of relative inactivity on the night of the 9th – a bitter night during which men at the front died from exposure – there was something more profound at fault. In warm offices, ten miles or more behind the front, the commanders and staffs of armies and corps seemed to doze, a large proportion undoubtedly going to bed at a time when there should have been an explosion of creative energy instead of a mere collation of information.

Nearer the front, with the members of Divisional and Brigade HQs, there was certainly much more activity though even they were mainly absorbed with internal reorganisation rather than the generation of transcendent pressures against the enemy. Apathy did not cause this torpor since, for the most part, the Commanders and their Staffs were men of good conscience – if only partially trained: the trouble lay rooted in their astonishment – a feeling of complete surprise at the speed and extent of the breakthrough. A mere six months before it had been impossible to achieve anything like this on the Somme, where ambitious targets had been set but never realised. Throughout 1916 everybody had become inured to advancing but a few hundred yards in a session and then taking a long pause to gather more artillery ammunition before stepping forward again. From a staff point of view it had been a comparatively leisurely process, easily calculable in time and space. Moreover, so constricted were horizons at the entrenched front, only Brigade Commanders and below had much chance directly to influence the battle. Then – suddenly on Vimy Ridge and at Arras – the whole vista changed. Ambitious objectives were instantly realised, the front burst open and everybody could suddenly move freely for the space of a few hours. It had become possible for army, corps and divisional leaders to watch everything moving into place, had they taken up a position to do so. But invariably they were too far away and too slow to appreciate the significance of events in order to take immediate advantage of opportunities. They lacked preconsidered battle drills for mobile war. Thus they hesitated to take direct control but instead looked over their shoulders for enlightened guidance that rarely came. And those orders which eventually arrived were usually either out of date or too late for effective implementation. Let us see how this lacuna stultified action on 10th April.

Haig, at the highest level of all, deferred making a suggestion of alternative 'approaches' to Allenby until 1030 hours on the 10th – perhaps because he preferred not to jostle a senior subordinate but just as likely because there was a long-standing antipathy between the two men. Neither general was at his best in conference and Allenby could be positively uncommunicative over large issues and, worse, at times explosive in his wrath over relatively trivial matters. At all events Haig's suggestion – that extra weight should be committed by the injection of 1st Cavalry Division north of the Scarpe, in addition to what Allenby already intended to the south – was too late to be of much help until the 11th. It took that much time to formulate and disseminate fresh orders. Allenby himself neither did much on the night of the 9th to vary his original instructions that laid down action for the 10th, nor felt the need to press his corps commanders any harder. It could be that a natural reticence inhibited a clear exposition of his thoughts. He might have been unprepared for such overwhelming success. At all events, Allenby seems to have assumed that the unprecedented progress achieved on the 9th would be extended automatically into the 10th and that, where time had been lost and objectives remained untaken, he could rely on his subordinates to catch up. Here he was wrong. If nothing more ambitious than tidying up was to take place on the Heights of Vimy – the capture of Point 145 by the Canadians and the final clearing of the line of the Ridge by 51st and 34th Divisions after their failure on the 9th – there was ample scope for extra pressure to be applied on either side of the Scarpe. Fergusson, commanding XVII Corps, was, for instance, in need of a boost. He talked small – merely of consolidating the objectives of the previous day. He delayed a further advance by 4th Division, first because only two of his seven artillery brigades had come up into range (he made no attempt to hurry them on the night of the 9th); then because of the need to await VI Corps coming up on the right (of which little was known); and finally to await the arrival of 1st Cavalry Brigade for a concerted attack upon Greenland Hill, the next key feature to his front.

Haldane did hardly any better with VI Corps to the south of the river. Information may have been extremely slow reaching his HQ but he made no great effort to impress an urgent, impulsive movement upon his divisional commanders. Yet Haldane was fully aware of the gap that had been created by 15th Division though ignorant of news (later confirmed by air contact patrols) that 63rd Brigade had entered it the previous night and virtually taken Orange Hill. Aggressive enquiries on his part throughout the night might have revealed, well before 1030 hours on the 10th, that this was the case. In that event he might have demanded something more dramatic than that which he did – a mere tidying up of untaken objectives on Orange Hill – which was, in any case, already largely his. So the gap in front of Monchy remained open and unexplored until mid-day when the leading elements of 63rd Brigade, waiting patiently all morning for orders, set off for this key objective which they could have had for the asking the night before, if not at dawn that day. Now, too, the mood of anticlimax was heightened by the artillery whose guns were only gradually occupying fresh advanced positions. They were inhibited by restrictions upon engaging German guns north of the river on Greenland Hill, by the fear that, since 1st Cavalry Division was known to be approaching that area, they might engage friend instead of foe. So formations working north of the river waited, in ignorance, for those to the south, and vice versa, while VI Corps' infantry advanced unsupported except for a bombardment of Monchy by heavy guns. Clearly there was a total failure at army and corps HQs to co-ordinate accurately their activities in a fast moving situation.

The Cavalry Corps, too, was appallingly slow in everything it did – but again it lacked firm directions and a thrusting policy. Some units, on returning from the front the previous night, did not reach their billets until 0300 hours. To expect them to be fit for action at the front by mid-morning – let alone by dawn – was therefore impossible. Thus Allenby's orders, that 2nd and 3rd Cavalry Divisions should be ready to advance south of the Scarpe after 0700 hours were at once meaningless. The best the horsemen could do was try to return to the eastern outskirts of Arras by noon and reach the vicinity of Chapel and Orange Hills by 1500 hours. Little daylight then remained and so 3rd Division's operation fizzled out. With them there was no urgency, no pounding desire to snatch the opportunity they had sought for two years. The long wait may, indeed, have sapped their resolve. It was true that this night 5th Cavalry Brigade opted to stick it out at the front, the men crouched in shell holes, holding their horses' bridles, risking the shelling in order to be ready for the dawn. But the rest drifted back into Arras.

Second Cavalry Division did hardly any better, making a dash in the afternoon for the spur connecting Monchy with Pelves, but, coming under heavy fire from Monchy and the undisturbed Germans on Greenland Hill, were saved only by a sudden snowstorm, blanketing them from view and from a terrible slaughter. That morning they could have gone through: that night it was too late.

So much more might have been achieved on a day when confusion was as rife in the German ranks as in the British. The full scale of the disaster of the 9th was only now beginning to dawn upon German comprehension. To various points on the front parts of reserve formations were dribbling up, but in a state of awful uncertainty and largely short of guns and ammunition. Ludendorff suffered a characteristic spasm of 'great depression' – as well he might. Rupprecht complained bitterly, and sacked Falkenhausen's Chief of Staff, though refusing Falkenhausen's own offer to resign. (It is often safer in an autocracy to let the public mind see justice done but to leave the godheads untouched – for a while.) Staff work went seriously awry under stress – the relief of 11th Infantry by 26th Infantry Division to the front of Monchy was a case in point. On the unauthorised order of a staff officer, the badly emaciated 11th Division evacuated the Monchy Line, though it was assumed they would continue to hold the village. But then, to make confusion doubly sure, it was erroneously reported that the 11th had abandoned Monchy too. So the impending relief by 26th Division, as it began to arrive, was amended by orders telling it instead to occupy and

Above: Means of mobility: the horses were softened by the winter
Below: The cavalry try to break through where the infantry has consolidated

Reinforcements arrive in London omnibuses

fortify 'the ridge next to it'. Thus an unwanted but involuntary retreat took place – and on a wide front too, since, at the same time, the pressure by British VII Corps in the south had impelled the withdrawal of 17th Reserve Division complete, bending back its flank where, on the 9th, it had secured the Hindenburg Line at Neuville Vitasse. All this took place as VII Corps began to advance again and as 63rd Brigade set off for Monchy. In consequence, though German reinforcements were actually arriving in some strength – 'a great arc of our batteries on a wide front behind our endangered positions' – the German front remained fluid, its occupants by no means as secure as they would have wished and the artillery ammunition shortage still acute. Nevertheless on the 10th the defence fixed a grip on the Scarpe between Monchy and Roeux – that key sector where security mattered most of all since it was here that the British were trying hardest in their attempts to exploit the penetrations of the previous day.

North of the river the British cavalry attack on Greenland Hill (the prospect of which had deterred its friendly artillery from bombarding the slopes) hung fire in a welter of indecision. The leading horsemen of 1st Cavalry Brigade failed to reach Fampoux until 1630 hours. At once their leader gave it as his opinion that mounted action was out of the question – an opinion strengthened by timely reports of an impending enemy counterattack which, in fact, was nothing more threatening than a readjustment of the German front. Simultaneously it began to snow and everybody happily agreed to call it a day, releasing the cavalry to ride safely back to Athies. They could hardly be blamed. One enemy machine gun would be more than enough for a squadron and an undisturbed enemy on Greenland Hill would be more than a match for this brigade even if all its ten squadrons got into action. Here 4th Division stood still throughout the day because Fergusson had not decreed a move, yet they alone, if they had been helped by the 9th Division and co-ordinated with VI Corps on the right, might have taken Greenland Hill with ease. In essence the British command fell asleep and step by step behind the Germans as they were stretching every fibre to restock an empty front with men and guns. Only with the minutae of trench warfare (which they understood) – up on the Heights of Vimy – did the British make any sort of sense that day.

To the north-west of Fampoux, 34th Division had still to complete the capture of the ridge at those places where it had been held back on the 9th due to the failure of 51st Division on their left. In fact they had little difficulty in doing so along most of their front, harvesting many more abandoned guns as they went. Only from Bailleul did hostile fire make difficulties. Indeed 34th reached the crest just in time to see a German battalion advancing in open order to reoccupy the ridge and were able to disperse it with well directed artillery fire – demonstrating, had it been necessary, how complete was British mastery on XVII Corps' front had Allenby and Fergusson decided to take advantage of it. Likewise where 152nd Brigade, from 51st Division, attacked in unison with 34th, the crest line was reached for the most part, the only setback coming from an all too obvious direction – that section of trench on the left of the division which 154th Brigade claimed they held when, in fact, they were merely occupying the communication trench at right angles. It was only now that General Harper came to believe what Currie had told him the previous day – that a wide gap lap open between the 34th and the Canadians, quite unfilled by his own 51st. But whereas on the 9th the 51st could have taken the ridge without opposition, they now had to fight for it and in fighting were to be twice repulsed. Furthermore, it was not until the evening of the 11th that they were actually allowed to get there – and then unopposed only because the Germans had quietly withdrawn. This was a maddening episode, particularly if we recall that, on the 9th, an officer with a section from 153rd Machine Gun Company had actually arrived in the line adjacent to the Canadian right, lugging his guns, their tripods and ammunition, and walked several yards southward down unoccupied trenches, shelled by his own artillery, but quite unmolested by the Germans who had fled. Next morning the enemy had returned – well in time to prepare a reception for the 51st.

None of this seems seriously to have affected the Canadians on the left of 51st Division. They were not asked to apply flank pressure in aid of 51st Division and seem to have been content to hold a protective flank while doing all in their power to repair communications leading to the crest as the essential prerequisite to dragging forward the guns and ammunition to support any further advance. In fact, by the evening of 10th April, all thought of exploiting the breakthrough of the 9th – even by strong patrols – had been abandoned. The most that might happen would be a formal attack in co-operation with the British – and not before the 13th. All that effort and expenditure of blood, yet now Horne and Byng let them stand still and watched the Germans rebuilding their front to such good purpose that, within days, it would require another full-scale bombardment before a man could advance.

Activity around Point 145 was, of course, intense, for this was the one outstanding enemy enclave left over from the 9th, which had to be cleared to make the heights wholly Canadian. Very wisely it had been decided to eject the Germans by a slow, meticulous plan instead of a rushed impro-

visation. The conditions of siege warfare still strictly applied in this sector, there was time to spare and no sense in causing avoidable bloodshed – except among the Germans. In any case the situation had become highly confused by nightfall on the 9th. Nobody knew how far some troops from 11th Brigade had got in the maze of trenches and therefore it was extremely difficult to 'place' the artillery fire without causing needless losses to friendly infantry. That the Germans were also showing promise of a counter-attack from the direction of the Pimple was certainly an incentive to haste, but it was resisted. Some Germans actually struggled their way to the Pimple, and then tried to cross the morass in the direction of Point 145, but they only lost their way, and their boots as well, as the mud sucked them off with every step they took. Bootless, it required but a single burst of machine gun fire to dissuade them from further adventure.

The second attempt to take Point 145 was to be undertaken by the 10th Brigade which, as the reserve formation in 4th Canadian Division, had been earmarked to take the Pimple that day. In consequence, the Pimple operation had to be postponed when two of 10th Brigade's battalions were given the work of cleaning up Point 145 behind a strong concentration of gunfire on the afternoon of the 10th. The approach by two battalions – 44th (Manitoba) and 50th (Calgary) – was deliberate and systematic, crossing the start line at 1500 hours and descending in a wild rush upon the Germans whose fire was desperate and accurate, though insufficient to save them from destruction. With bomb and bayonet the Canadians swept to the line of the crest, shot down in handfuls themselves, but quite unstoppable. Calgary Regiment lost 229 but liberated 150 of their own unwounded compatriots who had been held prisoner. Within half an hour they had achieved their objectives so

Above left: The guns take over again. *Above:* The heavies roar
Below: The 18-pounders crack

Above: Monchy dissolves. *Below:* Monchy after the battle

that, as darkness fell, 4th Canadian Division took possession of all that remained in German hands of Vimy Ridge. Now just Bois en Hâche and the Pimple remained to be dealt with, but these would have to wait until the 12th. In the meantime there were more significant matters to be resolved away to the south.

Twenty-four hours too late General Allenby began to take a rugged, personal grip on the battle at Arras. But his orders, issued on the evening of 10th April and reflecting Haig's desires of the morning, would have been more appropriate had they been given and executed on the evening of the 9th. He insisted upon all Corps closing up to the line which should have been reached on the 9th and demanded that VI and VII Corps should 'reach the Drocourt – Quéant Line' – some five miles ahead – or at almost twice the speed thus far achieved. His orders certainly reflected the mood of the 9th: 'The Army Commander wishes all troops to understand that Third Army is now pursuing a defeated enemy and that risks must be freely taken. Isolated enemy detachments in farms and villages must not be allowed to delay the general progress.' Mere words, these were, unfortunately. By the evening of the 10th the 'isolated enemy detachments' were being bound into a cohesive line, their centres of resistance such prominent features as Greenland Hill, Monchy and the ruins of the windmill (called Wancourt Tower by the British) on La Crête de Douai, overlooking Guémappe, and the main axis of advance along the Cambrai road. From these nodal points machine guns spat back defiance and the observers controlling a growing mass of artillery laid down their protective barrages.

Then again there was uncertainty in the actuation of Allenby's demands, for though he intended a general advance to begin at 0500 hours on the 11th, this was not made clear in Fergusson's VII Corps north of the Scarpe. So 4th Division, left to its own devices, delayed an attack until noon since the commander wanted a six hour preliminary bombardment. In due course 4th Division was to be stopped dead in the approaches to Roeux while 34th Division probed towards Gavrelle and 51st Division completed its occupation of the Ridge. Nothing more was to come from VII Corps that day. Likewise on XVII Corps' front attempts to seize Guémappe bogged down before the resistance that centred on Wancourt Tower. But up at Monchy, where the village overtopped the surrounding hills, there remained a morsel of progress to justify Allenby's claims.

Sixth Corps had as its principal objective the village – a task given to 37th Division, while 15th Division came up level on its left and 3rd Cavalry Division waited close by in rear to exploit. There was a muddle among the gunners, however, due to a reallocation of batteries in support of different formations, and delay in fresh orders reaching those of the infantry and tanks who were to take part. In consequence some of the infantry advanced without artillery support, and failed to make all their objectives, while those in 111th Brigade declined to advance at all until the gunners could meet their commitments – thus delaying their start from 0500 to 0700. But this far from suited three tanks which had wended their way forward in the dark and now stood exposed to view on a bare slope, silhouetted against the snow, well knowing that once dawn had broken they would be the target for every German gun in sight. For these tanks the only cover available was to the front – in Monchy and thence they made their own way in the pious hope that the infantry would follow in due course.

Monchy was only just beginning to suffer the effects of intensive bombardment, for until the 10th it had been the recipient of little more than scattered attention. Therefore the streets and the central square, though their buildings burnt, were almost uncluttered by rubble. So the tanks had a relatively easy passage the length of the place. German infantry reaction at first was that of panic – a scramble for safety in cellars and down side streets as the three monsters clanked ponderously by. It was not until they had traversed the entire place and emerged in isolated splendour beyond that the local garrison woke up to the fact that these machines were on their own. Hence, when the tanks returned in response to aggressive noises from within the village, there was a reception waiting. Now, as the three tanks took up a stand in the village square, German anti-tank measures came into play – '. . . while bundles of hand-grenades are thrown against the tank tracks – without success. Useless also the daring attempts to climb the tanks in order to shoot through openings and flaps or to force explosives into them'. Eventually it was to be armour-piercing bullets, fired by a machine gun from an upstairs window, which silenced first one and then a second tank, leaving the third in only tenuous possession of the square. But now at last it was time for the formal British artillery barrage to begin, preceding the infantry assault, to turn the village into an holocaust – wrecking the surviving tank and putting the Germans to flight.

From three directions British infantry appeared, some from 15th Scottish moving through on their way to Pelves, others from 111th Brigade taking cover in cellars as desultory German artillery fire now descended with a crash. And into the midst rode a splendid sight – two regiments of cavalry, endeavouring to find shelter from fire which swept the northern side of the village and coming under yet more fire as they attempted to exit to the east: finally to be driven to dismount and fight as infantry in a line all too thinly held. Thus, though no German attack was forthcoming

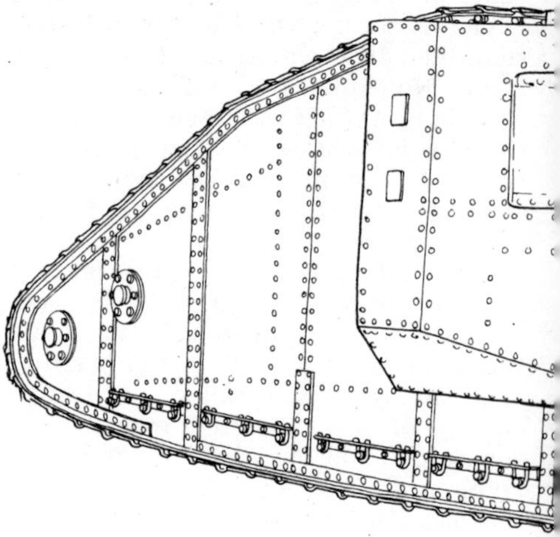

(it was discussed by their command but found impossible to implement) and both sides' artillery raged on and about the village, progress was at an end. The guns had taken over, the gap filled by Germans in possession of a solid line once more, though positioned much farther to the east than they would have liked.

Monchy was an important capture and marked the first successful action by tanks on their own – even if an involuntary one. Tanks had more deliberately tried to work on their own much further south, in Fifth Army sector between Quéant and Bullecourt. Here the exuberant General Gough, high in Haig's favour, made an effort to apply flank pressure against the Hindenburg Line proper and widen the frontage of British penetration. With little time for preparation, it was decided to attempt a surprise attack with twelve tanks without a preliminary bombardment – a worthy idea which ran into confusion because of inadequate pre-battle training, several misunderstandings and a series of mechanical failures. Be that as it may, the Australian infantry, who were intending to follow the assault, found themselves, after a postponement, committed to an assault in which the tanks, by loss or

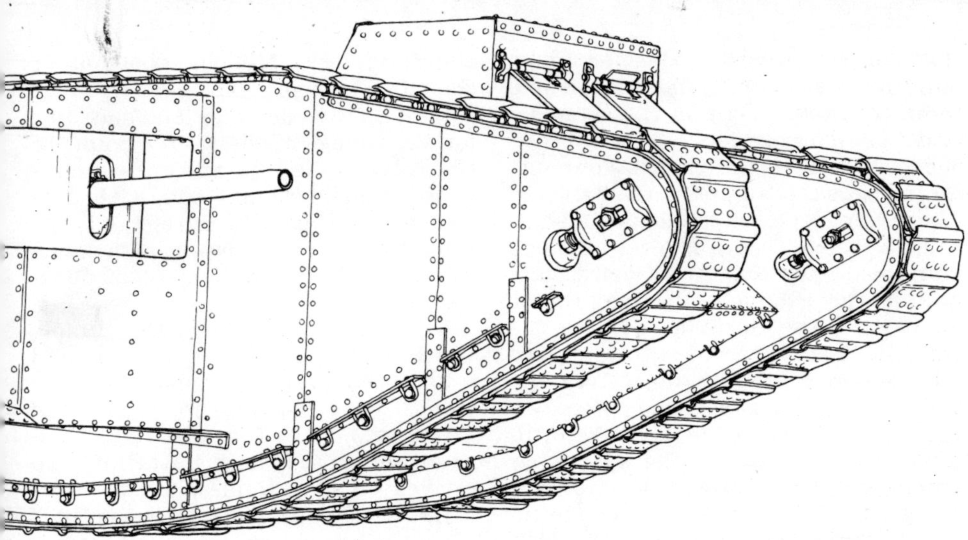

Tanks were first used on the Somme in September 1916, part of a small production batch. The latest types were not ready on April 1917 and therefore those tanks used at Arras were the original Mark I with tail-wheels renewed. Armour was low grade and badly pointed. Crew control was rudimentary and it took four men to steer and change gear. *Weight:* 28 tons. *Crew:* 8. *Armament:* two long-barrelled naval 6-pounder guns and provision for three 8-mm Hotchkiss machine guns. *Armour:* none as such, but the construction was in boiler plate, which was replaced by armour in the Mark I. *Power:* Daimler water-cooled inline, 105hp. *Speed:* 3.7 mph maximum. *Trench crossing:* 9 feet. *Step:* 4 feet 6 inches. *Range:* 50 miles maximum. *Length:* 26 feet 5 inches. *Height:* 8 feet 2 inches. *Width:* 13 feet 9½ inches.

absence, were to play little constructive part. Liaison with the artillery was uniformly poor and so, in a confused situation, the Australians were largely deficient of any sort of support, especially when a local gunner commander doubted the wisdom of firing close to where the Australians were supposed to be. Eventually there was a total repulse in which 4th Australian Brigade was wiped out.

This disaster, coming on top of conclusive evidence of an *impasse* along the length of Third Army's front, convinced Allenby that the time for 'taking risks' had passed. In any case the troops who had assaulted so strongly on the 9th were now utterly spent and in need of immediate relief by fresh formations – which could only be supplied with Haig's permission. For the 12th Allenby set less ambitious objectives, maintaining the pressure but abandoning hope of reaching the Drocourt Quéant Switch, let alone Cambrai. And if this day Haig confirmed to the French (who were still four days away from their attack on the Chemin des Dames) that Cambrai was still the objective, this was no longer within the bounds of feasibility – as he must have known.

Events on the 12th, in addition to assuring the doom of the Nivelle offensive as a whole, also marked the final stage of the battle for the Vimy Heights – the attack by the British 73rd Brigade on Bois en Hâche and Canadian 10th Brigade on the Pimple. Both were to begin at 0500 hours and at a stroke would wrest the last elements of high ground from German possession. But it was not only the immensity of the preliminary artillery bombardment which would make sure of success. The Germans here were in dire trouble, undernourished, cold, depressed, thin on the ground – and awaiting orders to withdraw. Only the soil was in their favour – so waterlogged that the Canadians on the lower slopes were clogged advancing a bare 100 yards every fifteen minutes. Thus they were delayed in taking the Pimple and gave greater scope to those Germans holding the Bois en Hâche to take toll of 73rd Brigade. But at both objectives the end was inevitable. The pre-dawn gloom, made darker by a snowstorm, gave partial cover to the advancing infantry who, on entering the German trenches, found an enemy in no condition to resist at length. Men who crouched dismally in shell holes were only too pleased to surrender. Indeed in places, where no trenches or shell holes existed, the Germans of 4th Guard Division (who had but just arrived) merely huddled in the mud and made no attempt to resist. By mid-morning the matter was closed on a note of triumph, but which, in many ways, had a hollow sound.

Some two days before it was plain to the Germans that to counterattack was impossible and to remain close under the heights ridiculous. Falkenhausen, bowing to Rupprecht's orders that an intermediate line of defence was to be held on the line Méricourt – Arleux – Gavrelle – Pelves and thence to the east of Monchy, had been slow to abandon his earlier desire to counterattack the heights, but the final ejection from Point 145 on the 10th left him with no alternative. On the 11th there was a meeting at Tournai between Falkenhausen, his new Chief of Staff, Colonel von Lossberg, and Rupprecht's Chief of Staff, General von Kuhl. After that orders were issued for the withdrawal to take place on the night of the 12th. This Rupprecht justified to Ludendorff: 'After the defeat of April 9th . . . an improvement in the present position can only be possible by a systematic retreat. . . .' But even a stand on the Gavrelle – Monchy position he considered a mere expedient – '. . . it cannot be considered as a defence line for very long. A possibility could be the Pelves – Vis – Quéant line which is under construction'. And with this Ludendorff gloomily agreed, at the same time fearing renewed attacks on the flanks of the broken sector opposite Vimy.

So on 12th April when the Pimple and Bois en Hâche were assailed and taken, the first echelon of German troops were already in process of thinning out the front, and the Canadian sergeant in 44th Battalion who arrived on the Pimple and saw 'German limbers galloping to the rear down the Lens Arras road' was simply observing the opening stage of a formal withdrawal.

Already adept at making a clean break from contact, the Germans made no mistakes worthy of note on the night of the 12th. Of course, had a projected Canadian move to occupy the Bailleul – Vimy railway materialised on the night of the 10th the Germans might have been caught badly off balance but, as it was, the Canadians lay dormant throughout the night of the 12th, watching flares rising to their front, ducking routine bursts of fire shot in their direction – suffering in essence, the normal backfirings of any other trench night. Not until daylight was it realised that the German front line was empty, though patrols were soon reporting deserted trenches and fires were seen burning in dug-outs in the direction of Lievin. At once Byng ordered a general advance by strong patrols that dodged stealthily forwards, always fearing a trap. They advanced throughout the afternoon towards great fires at Lens and Avion which told of extensive demolition of articles the Germans could not remove in time. Quantities of wrecked guns, stores and equipment, plus a few prisoners, were picked up – indicative of the forced nature of the German withdrawal. But nowhere could there be hope of throw-

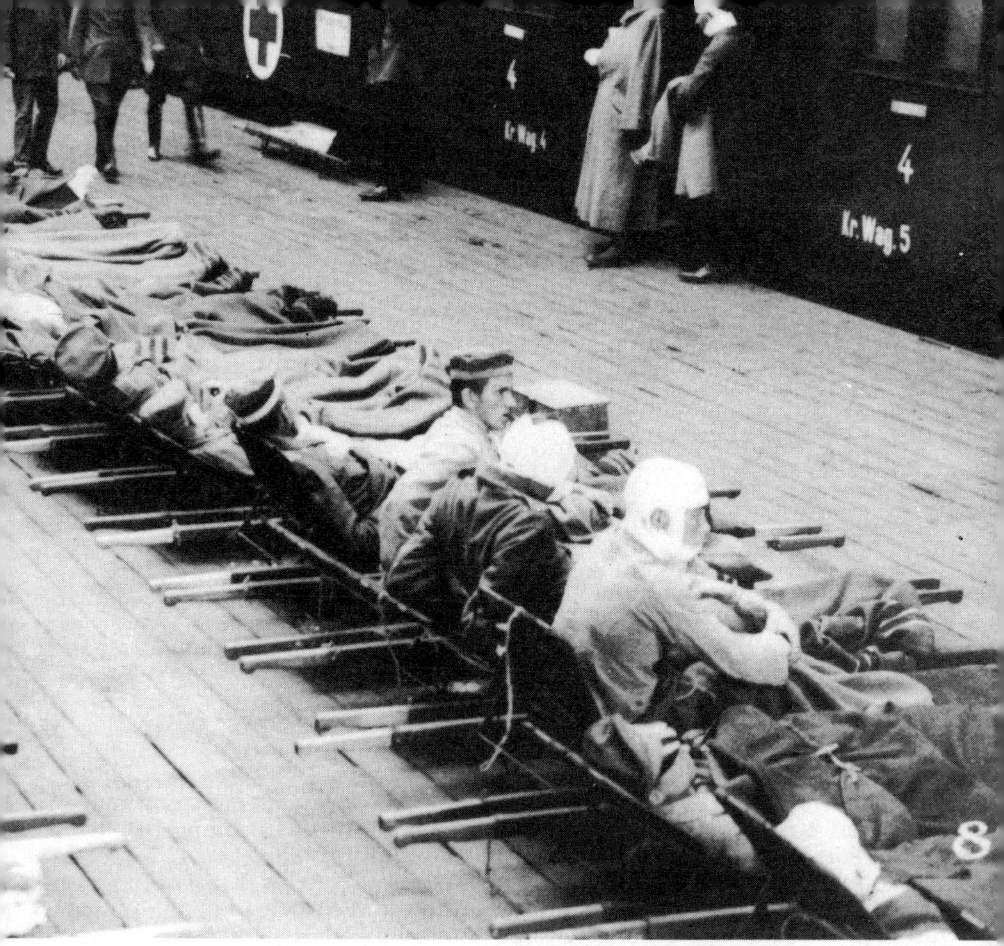

ing the Germans into disorder. By the 14th, in fact, it was the Canadians' turn to start digging in at a disadvantage on fresh ground, somewhat exposed for a while to better entrenched Germans and no longer so well off for observation as they had been from the crest of the Ridge. Indeed the journey down the Ridge face was a most harrowing business at all times, as those guns first sent down to establish themselves in Vimy came under constant bombardment. Ammunition supply too had its problems there, as one gunner tells. 'We started out with two wagons, but getting near the top of the ridge there were some dead horses on the side of the road. We tried our best to get past them but the horses just stopped and the mules lay down in the road . . . Then the Germans started shelling the road, some coming quite close and the horses became unmanageable and ditched the wagons . . .'

The old routine was reasserting itself – the toilsome business of survival, knock and knock, with scarce an advantage to one side or the other. The euphoria of the 9th would evaporate, soon lost almost in its entirety to British regard. But forever it would be famous in Canadian annals. The Nivelle offensive, however, would go on – now at Arras, then on the Chemin des Dames and, thereafter, who could tell where?

Return traffic to Germany

The breaking strain

The problem facing General Haig on 14th April was that of a man impaled on the points of a trident; hooked by the obligation of supporting the French ally to whom he had promised full support in a major offensive but who, on the 13th, had further postponed his attack until the 16th; caught by anxiety to save his men from unavailing losses in a wilting battle; spurred to revert to his own offensive designs in Flanders. For General Allenby, in the meantime, there was the unenviable prospect of fighting a battle of the fly against the web, each diminishing effort to break free from the strengthened German defences leading to closer bondage and eventual suffocation. On 12th April Allenby had endeavoured to conserve his strength while maintaining the pressure deemed necessary to divert German attention from the French. He asked only that limited objectives should be tackled and in a strict order of precedence – first the high ground to the east of Wancourt, then the village of Roeux and later, perhaps, a drive towards Vis past Guémappe. He copied, for want of something better, the French pattern as it had been on Vimy Ridge and elsewhere in 1915. Once the clear-cut reality of a breakthrough had passed there came a reversion to the nightmare of attritional warfare. Thus the battles of 13th April and 14th were to be disjointed, costly and abortive, those taking place to the east of Monchy classics of disorder.

Attempts to seize Wancourt Tower quickly failed and consequently the chances of occupying Guémappe became remote. Moreover the relief of the worn out divisions was occurring in close contact with the enemy, in haste, and within poorly defined boundaries. Indeed, for 29th Division, taking over from 37th Division before Monchy, it would be impossible for their right flank brigade (87th) to be ready to attack eastwards on the 14th. Nevertheless, the 88th Brigade, on the division's left, reckoned that it would be ready. So regardless of the lack of co-operation with its neighbours, it thrust forward out of Monchy at dawn on the 14th, making for the gap between Bois du Sart and Bois du Vert, hoping that the enemy in Guémappe would stay ineffective under close artillery fire. The sheer fantasy of this seemingly paltry British assault by a mere two battalions, albeit heavily supported by fire, seems to have stupified the Germans by its audacity. At all events their front gave way and for a fleeting moment a repetition of events on the 9th were to be seen. For the men of the 1st Essex Regiment and the Royal Newfoundland Regiment it must indeed have seemed miraculous that so small a force as theirs could drive a wedge 1,000 yards deep into the enemy lines with so few casualties to themselves, securing a mass of prisoners at a stroke. By 0700 hours they found themselves in the open on a small hill between the two woods – two lonely units with nowhere to go and nobody left behind in Monchy to protect their rear or provide reinforcements.

Now came the sort of counterattack such as the new German system of 'elastic' defence prescribed and which, until then, had been all too rare in execution. Their companies which had survived, lying in rear and to the flanks of the British penetration, began, on their own initiative, to close in upon the little salient, a haphazard constriction by a series of local infiltrations culminating in what the British, caught unconsolidated, must have judged to be a carefully prepared trap. The collapse of what, but a few moments before, had been two well ordered and triumphant battalions became, therefore, all the more complete. And now the Germans, swept onward by enthusiasm, pursued their beaten enemy to the outskirts of Monchy, little thinking that the place, now under light German shellfire, was theirs for the asking.

So it would have been had not the

General Lossberg

Commanding Officer of Royal Newfoundland Regiment, as he walked through the centre of the ruined village, become aware that, instead of his own men covering the ground to the east, it was German infantry who were within rifle shot of the houses. Thus Lieutenant-Colonel J Forbes-Robertson found himself with but eight men to hold the village, his best hope of reinforcement the chance that his Adjutant had escaped to the rear to find help. Forbes-Robertson and his little band now took post in a trench and for over four hours shot down every German who tried to advance. Reinforcements were on their way, though delayed by German shelling to the west of the village. Yet this very gunfire was as much the cause of the German infantry halting as Forbes-Robertson's party, for the German gunners, unaware of their infantry's *ad hoc* counterattack, were merely maintaining a defensive barrage designed to prevent British reinforcement of 88th Brigade's original attack. The delay imposed was fatal, however, to any further German improvisations, for now, as British defensive gunfire mounted to a tumult in its endeavour to seal the approaches to the village, the German fire faltered: the ammunition railhead at Vitry had just come under long-range fire and ammunition trains were being stopped further back, thus depriving local stocks of sufficient reserve ammunition except for emergencies.

Something new in trench warfare was beginning to emerge from this strange compound of artillery dominance mixed with the new German elastic tactics – a *modus operandi* whereby one side or the other, by launching a local attack, could tempt enemy reserves into the open and expose them to a crushing artillery riposte – a cat and mouse game, not in the least likely to lead to a decision but ruinously expensive in life. This was to be the motif of the next round–the so-called Second Battle of the Scarpe.

It is unlikely, however, that this analysis percolated to Haig or that the ramshackle quality of Third Army's conduct of the battle on 14th April influenced his resolve to take direct charge of the offensive in person. Haig's decision to co-ordinate the activities of First, Third and Fifth Armies, taken as it was well before the end of the day, was dictated as much by external as by internal events. He most wanted to keep up pressure yet he also required a temporary pause to enable adequate preparation of simultaneous attacks along the length of a three-army frontage – a restatement of polic which cut across Allenby's interim piecemeal attacks but fell into line with a 'Resolution' submitted by three divisional commanders from VI Corps. Allenby let it be known that he agreed with the Resolution. What else could he do when Haig gave such scant attention to his views – possibly, it has been suggested, because Haig saw in Allenby a contender for his own post?

On the eve of Nivelle's attack against the Chemin des Dames Haig was planning to renew the offensive on the 20th, using First Army and its Canadians to attempt a breach of the line between Acheville and Oppy: Third Army would take the next row of hills east of Monchy and Fifth Army would chime in again near Bullecourt. By then it was hoped the French army would be in full flood northwards, loosening German resistance and resolve as they came. Indeed, even as the three army commanders sat in conference, the French stepped off on a venture which was to make or break many a reputation.

The basic trouble with Nivelle's offensive was always its lack of both strategic and tactical surprise, falling as it did upon an enemy thoroughly forewarned and well poised to resist – an opponent whose troops, moreover, had enjoyed just sufficient time to grasp the meaning and actuation of elastic defence. Despite the defeat at Arras the Germans had been able to

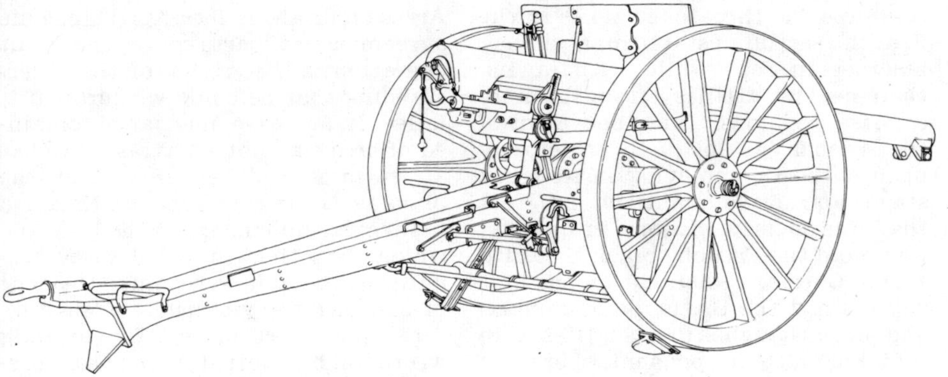

The French 75mm field gun, France's equivalent to the 18-pounder, was one of the world's great guns, and the French had an almost religious faith in its capabilities, which were very good. It was easy to fire and maintain, and was extremely accurate. *Calibre:* 75mm. *Weight of shell:* 16 pounds (shrapnel). *Weight of gun and carriage:* 2,657 pounds. *Range:* 7,440 yards. *Elevation:* —10° to +19°. *Rate of fire:* six rounds per minute was normal, but in desperate situations it was not unknown for crews to fire at the rate of twenty rounds per minute

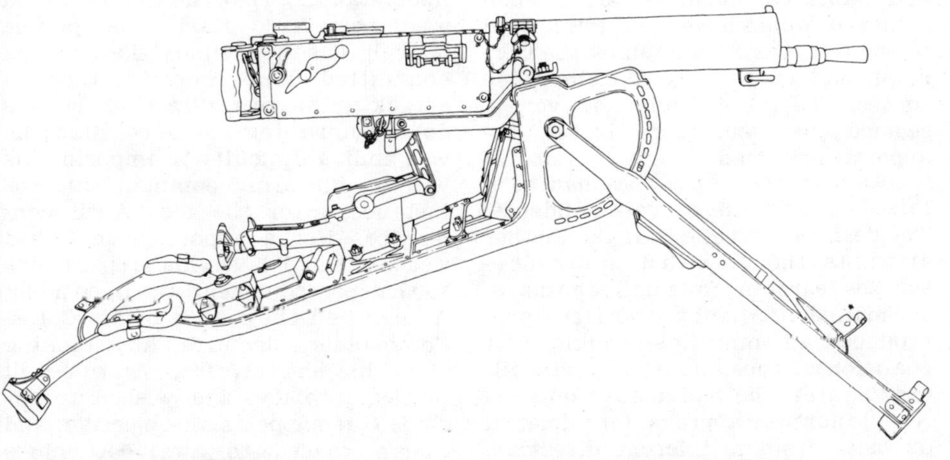

The German MG '08 heavy machine gun. This weapon was the Germany army's standard heavy machine gun in the First World War, and was introduced, as its name suggests, in 1908. It was manufactured at the arsenal at Spandau near Berlin. The gun was based on the Maxim, and its action was essentially the same as that of the British Vickers machine gun. The original sleigh type mounting was very heavy, and a lightened version was introduced in 1915. *Calibre:* 7.92mm. *System:* Recoil, automatic only. *Length of gun:* $46\frac{1}{4}$ inches. *Length of barrel:* $28\frac{1}{4}$ inches. *Coolant:* Water. *Feed:* 100- and 250-round fabric belts. *Muzzle velocity:* 2,750 feet per second. *Rate of fire:* 400 to 500 rounds per minute. *Weight of gun:* $40\frac{1}{2}$lbs. *Weight of mount:* 83lbs ($65\frac{1}{2}$lbs 1915 mount)

reinforce the threatened zones in the French sector, establishing strong reserves in rear while withdrawing their heavier artillery from its more exposed positions. Thus the weight of the French attack fell principally upon outposts, achieving in its early stages attractive quantitive progress that was mostly illusory in quality. Never did the French breach the third line of German resistance on the first day (as had the British at Fampoux) and, even though stiff casualties were inflicted on their opponent, there was no crisis or a splitting open of the front such as had been achieved by the British. In due course well over 10,000 prisoners and 187 guns were to be taken – many as the result of a panicky and involuntary German withdrawal on one threatened sector – but French casualties in ten day's fighting were to amount to nearly 100,000, magnified by a breakdown in medical organisation to the cruel detriment of the wounded. Advances and captures, such as the French achieved, would have been trumpeted to the world as a triumph by the Germans had they enjoyed comparable success. To the French, however, it seemed just one more bitter disappointment made worse by natural reaction to the hopes that had been raised by Nivelle's over-confidence. The desire by Nivelle to make further attempts, though with diminished resources searching for smaller gains, in the manner of Allenby after 11th April, produced an immediate backlash. A coalition of those political and military figures who had always opposed Nivelle now won approval for a delayed offensive from a different direction. But even this mood was transitory, for next came signs of unrest in the ranks of French soldiery, a rot which was to spread and threaten something worse than the loss of just another battle.

Haig, thoroughly apprised of Nivelle's failure, and soon to be aware of his French opposite number's loss of credibility, would have been perfectly justified in stopping the offensive at Arras on or about 18th April since his agreement to partake in the joint operation had been based on the understanding that he could withdraw if it failed. In any case, no chance remained of breaking out at Arras now that all surprise had been lost. But the plans agreed in conference by Haig and his army commanders on the 16th, and which were then intended to be actuated on the 20th, were laid in the hope of meeting the victorious French on their northward march, for, as Haig wrote in his despatch, he was prepared to continue at Arras 'until such time as the results of the French offensive declared themselves'.

By the 20th it was just conceivable that the French would be still in the attack business, but by the time Haig became aware, on the 18th, that the British attack would also be delayed, the chances of serious French participation were waning. Nivelle was reduced to making a request for continued British attacks on the poignant understanding that the French would also persevere. Haig was pliable though it is more likely that, having committed himself to a renewed attack at his own direction, he was doubly unwilling to cancel since he was finding difficulty in imposing his will on his army commanders. For instance, after the 16th April conference, Horne reported that bad weather had delayed his preparations so that postponement was inevitable; Allenby, on the advice of his Corps' Commanders, demurred at attacking along his entire front, regardless of tactical probity, and wished to exclude Guémappe as an objective; and Gough wished to await Allenby's attack before moving himself. Eventually the offensive was retarded until the 23rd, Third Army was allowed to attack piecemeal and Gough permitted to help only with artillery fire. Unbriefed themselves, the army commanders had misled Haig; unsure of his authority and uncertain of the real situation at the front, Haig bowed to anarchy while reluctant to cancel

since this would be admission of personal weakness. Yet, on a later occasion, similar compromises were to attend Haig's attempts to get all three Armies to attack in unison. When Gough wanted to attack in the dark (at the instigation of his Australians) Horne and Allenby, doubtful of the proficiency of their men, wished to attack at dawn. Eventually Haig had them attack in unison but the start time was fixed for shortly before dawn, a compromise which satisfied nobody.

As French resolve slackened and Haig received reports of their disinclination to renew attacks on a large scale, he foresaw the need to maintain any sort of pressure against the Germans while in the process of switching his efforts to Flanders. Hence his offensive of 23rd April, and all that followed, essentially became diversions – fighting for fighting's sake with no tangible object in sight. For nearly a month the old tyranny of combat for limited objectives was to raise the casualty bill, lop off many of the best men who had improved their craft at Vimy and Arras, and weaken the armies to no real gain. Without going into a trench by trench commentary on each day's sordid grapple, it is sufficient to sense the atmosphere by vignettes.

There are stories of individual tanks, some offered for slaughter in isolation, others scoring notable successes on their own. Almost as if it were a sideshow for the benefit of the onlookers on the 23rd, a gunner officer in 50th Division recorded, 'It was a very exciting day . . . Our Division had a tank, and the first thing I could see, after the smoke had cleared, was the tank in flames'. After that he could concentrate on the real work in hand – the pummelling of German counter-attack infantry as they formed up in blocks. But another tank, working solo near Roeux, dominated the front and was virtually decisive in helping the infantry reach their objectives.

Failures: the cavalry are out of a job

As of right and might the guns of both sides dictated the battle, but in a contest wherein the German inferiority of 9th April was rapidly ameliorated. If, on the 9th, German Sixth Army could face British First and Third Armies with only 1,016 to 2,817 guns, by the 23rd it was in the proportion 1,329 to 2,685 and on 3rd May 1,421 to 2,685. An old exuberance re-energised the German gunners as recounted by one of their number as his battery took on a visible target in open ground: 'This is the moment when the heart of the artilleryman beats faster; this the moment when every gunner and every single man, whether he hauls the shells or fires them, becomes one of a co-ordinated device, one perfect machine, and with joy in his eyes sees the success of his exhausting labours . . . Go at it as hard as you can! That's it and again and again! Fire! Hurrah! With a wide sweep the battery skims the crest – bang – right in the middle! Target! – and force the English to ground.' And in more sombre tone the description by Ernst Jünger, a German infantryman under Canadian fire in the village of Fresnoy: '. . . The shells were sending up the earth in fountains as high as church towers. Each seemed bent on outdoing its predecessor. As though by magic one house after another was sucked into the earth. Walls collapsed, gables fell and bare rafters were flung through the air to mow the roofs of neighbouring houses. Clouds of splinters danced above whitish swathes of vapour. Eye and ear hung as though entranced upon this dance of destruction.'

Fresnoy was, indeed, the village towards whose capture the Canadians had bent every effort since 28th April when Currie's 1st Division had put in a dawn assault and cleaned out the Arleux loop in just two hours well rehearsed assault. So swift had been the attack on Arleux, so well reinforced once it reached its objectives

Cannon fodder

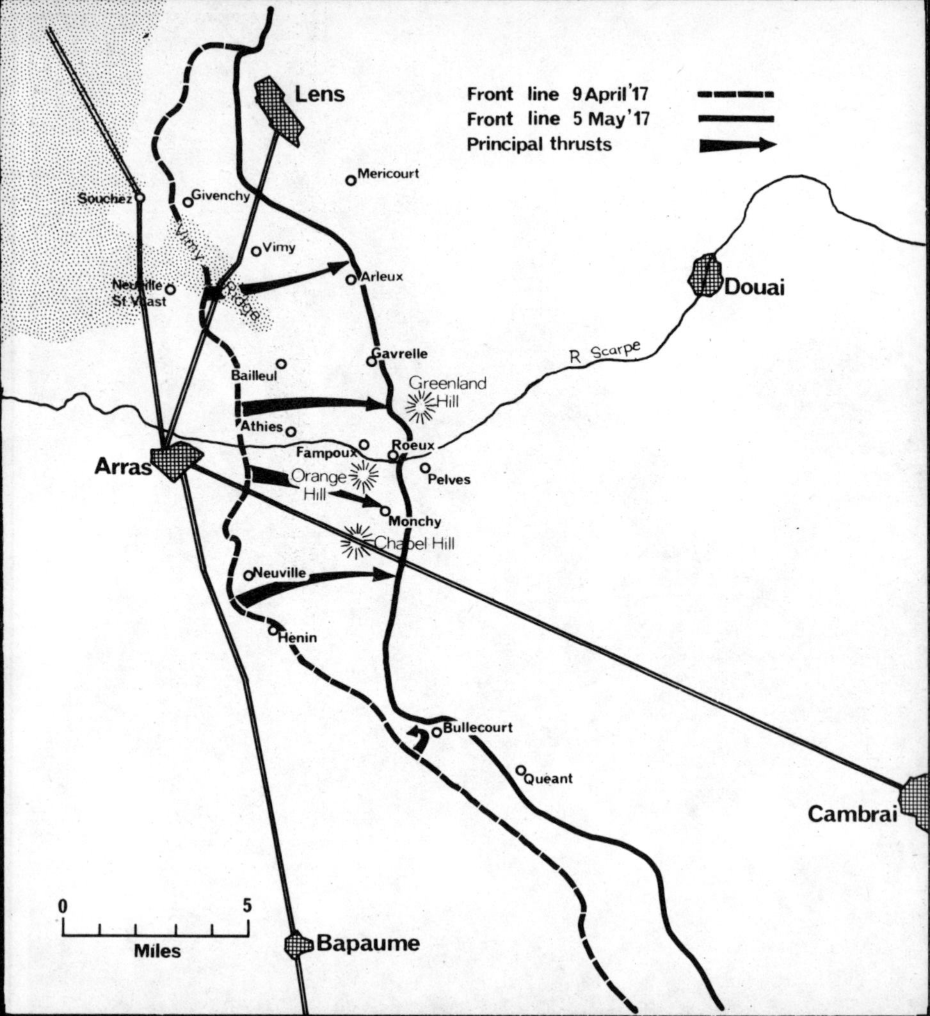

Canadian and British gains, 9th April to 5th May 1917

Fampoux after the battle

beyond the village and so thoroughly planned the curtain of gunfire brought down to seal off penetration by the routine German counterattack, that the latter hardly showed signs of starting. Indeed it was cancelled by the commander of German 111th Division once the strength of the Canadian penetration had been assessed along with the realisation that such an exposed position was not worth the retaking.

Thus Fresnoy took part in the front line as part of the defence in depth which was now being developed in Sixth Army under the guidance of Colonel von Lossberg. Lossberg, as it happened, was far from an enthusiastic addict of the 'elastic' defence, but rather favoured a flexible utilisation of successive entrenchments containing 'battle zones' in which the enemy should be obliterated by fire and judicious counterattacks. He abhorred the system of 'fortifications' such as had failed on Vimy Ridge and intended instead to hold two layers of Battle Zones to the west of the Drocourt Quéant Switch which, at last, was being developed along the lines of the Hindenburg Line and linked with what remained of that system in the vicinity of Quéant.

But on 3rd May, with the same precision as had attended the assault on Arleux, Currie struck at Fresnoy – this time gaining surprise with a night attack that found its way through gaps torn in the wire and caught the Germans unprepared. Here and there, notably on the left where 6th Brigade from 2nd Division lost direction, there was to be a partial rebuff and the taking of ground only as the result of superb examples of courage by individuals in the face of withering machine-gun fire. One officer, R G Combe, won a VC before he was killed, taking 250 yards of trench with the use of British and then German grenades. But, on the right, 1st Brigade rapidly swept the village clear, one of its companies actually penetrating the German lines and then reversing through 180 degrees to beat backwards, driving the Germans towards the rest of the Canadian battalion like beaters in a partridge shoot. At Fresnoy, regardless of cost, the Germans felt bound to counterattack, for its loss threatened this entire part of the Battle Zone. As they said, 'a stone had been knocked out of the German defensive wall which had to be replaced without delay'. And all

that day they tried to replace it, storming forward, for the loss of more than a thousand men, amidst an impenetrable barrage of Canadian artillery, machinegun and rifle fire. This sort of premeditated counterattack could be a most costly business once it became a matter of unexceptional routine, as neither Canadians, British nor French were slow to exploit when they realised that, by taking a vital place at low cost, they could force the Germans into automatic suicide.

In a welter of attritional warfare at its worst the Nivelle Offensive ground to its foreseeable end. Territorially the Allies had gained but one feature of lasting value – Vimy Ridge – and had relieved an important route centre – Arras – from a state of partial seige. The cost to the Allies (including those on the French front in the south) was some 250,000 casualties: to the Germans – always impossible to state with accuracy – about 210,000. All, with the exception of the taking of the Ridge, would soon be forgotten in the whirlwind of intensified war and shattering collapse of nations that would follow. Quickest of all to change would be those whose names were linked with failure and success. Already Lossberg had replaced Nagel on the German side and Falkenhausen was soon to go – moved to the post of Governor General of Belgium. Ludendorff had demonstrated his instability when under pressure – but this was barely heeded at the time and he had much to contribute in the next eighteen months. On the Allied side it was Nivelle who went first – his meteoric rise plunged into reverse as soon as the hollowness of his promises was exposed, his replacement by Pétain a matter of vital necessity in the trauma of a wildly fluctuating political situation in which the army fell into disrepute. For on 25th April had appeared the first positive signs of unrest in the French army and, on the 29th, outright rebellion by a few units as the harbinger of more widespread disaffection to come. The French army's reputation was as near being lost as it had in 1870. To those in the know France lay on the verge of emulating Russia and it would take a soldier with the confidence of the Government and the army to restore order and resuscitate combat spirit. This would be Pétain's main task to the exclusion of further offensives. Thus the torch had to be handed to the British who, alone on either side, were in a state to take the initiative in battle. For the rest nearly three years' endeavour had sieved courage down to the dregs of endurance.

While Haig's prestige (like Ludendorff's) remained unassailable, it appeared to some (including the victim himself) that Allenby paid the penalty for his failure to break out. Suddenly, early in June, he was summoned home to England and told to make preparations for a journey to Egypt to take command of the Expeditionary Force there. It is more likely, however, that when Robertson, the CIGS, put the suggestion to Lloyd George, the Prime Minister, he not only had in mind the selection of a man best suited to putting drive into a failing campaign in Palestine, but also the need to part Allenby from Haig to save further friction. In due course Allenby would demonstrate against the Turks the lessons he had learnt from his failure at Arras – how he could exploit breakthroughs by ruthless cavalry pursuits to take Jerusalem and, one day, hound the Turks into submission at Aleppo.

In Allenby's place to command Third Army would come the successful leader of the Canadian Corps – Byng. And in Byng's place, to command the Canadians, one of their own – the vibrant Arthur Currie, whose 1st Division had shown such drive and adaptability on Vimy Ridge and beyond. Thus a wholesale command shake-up followed the abortive April battles, changes which were to effect deeply the culminating stages of the war.

General Currie

Pendulum

The year 1917 which had begun so enticingly well for Allied hopes of final victory and, for the Germans, with the deepest mistrust of the future, confounded all prophecy, for it ended with the Allies in gravest difficulties and disarray and the Germans buoyed up by unexpected visions of a solution to all their problems. It was true, on the German side, that the U-Boat offensive had achieved nothing like the high expectations of its supporters, but landward defensive successes, judicious offensives and political upheavals had worked miracles of change. The British, persevering throughout the summer with unrewarding and expensive head-on attacks at Ypres against unyielding German trenches and pill-boxes, had been forced to witness the Allies of yesteryear falter and defect. France held fast but only in passive mood as Pétain effected repairs to the damage caused by the army's mutiny: Italy barely survived the débacle of Caporetto and, in recovering, syphoned off precious Anglo-French forces which, in essence, represented the remaining Allied reserve; Rumania and Russia were knocked out of the war altogether, thereby releasing vast German resources, which had been locked up on the Eastern Front, to flood through to the West and upturn the balance of forces. Almost overnight German strategic thinking could be reversed from a policy of defence in 1917 to one of aggression for 1918.

Yet, for all the additional manpower made available to the Germans for attack and despite a diminution of fighting men in the Allied order of battle (caused by a multiplicity of factors, both economical and political), the issues in battle continued to hinge upon the application of material – despite Ludendorff's ingenuous disclaimer of such a notion. Both sides knew well how to orchestrate massed guns. As a matter of routine they could deliver enormous tonnages of high-explosive and gas shells upon each other with deadly accuracy, increased flexibility of response to changing situations and, more important still, a numbing compression of effort in time and space. At Riga a German artillerist called Bruchmüller had won the battle at outset by making a surprise concentration of unregistered gunfire fall on an all but unexpectant Russian enemy. The one British victory of importance in 1917 had been won at Cambrai, not only because tanks were used in mass and by surprise for the first time (breaching the Hindenburg Line with ease)

Marshal Foch

Germany's March offensive: the masses prepare

but because the accompanying fire of 1,000 guns had neutralised the defences despite withholding their fire until the advance began. At last the methods so dear to Allenby and Holland the previous April had been expanded and allowed to prove their feasibility. But as yet nobody had demonstrated ways to accompany the advancing infantry and cavalry with a continuous volume of heavy artillery support beyond the first three miles. Most of the guns which fired in an initial barrage were soon left behind, unable to advance into or be supplied across the wasteland of their own creation.

Nevertheless, Russia's withdrawal from the war in December, allied to improved tactical methods, encouraged Ludendorff in the belief that the key to a solution was his. He would aim, for the first time, at the destruction of the British army as a whole, leaving the French for later digestion. Throughout the winter months he would roll men, guns and munitions into France to gain a temporary preponderance such that he hoped would decide the issue before the Americans arrived, later that year, in irresistable strength. He devised nine successive operational projects of which 'Michael' was to be first and greatest, committing, as it did, seventy-four divisions between Arras and La Fère, on 21st March, supported on a sixty-mile frontage by no less than 6,473 guns, concentrated secretly close behind the lines prior to unleashing their fire in unison a mere five hours before the assault.

Three principal factors encouraged the Germans in thinking they might win the trench war when everybody else had lost in the past. They believed that dense artillery fire, spread wide and far into the enemy defences, would effect a deep breach of the front and that this was all the more likely to occur if it was directed principally

against the weakest sectors in the Allied line. They next postulated that exploitation and the subsequent phase of mobility could best be maintained by the avoidance of enemy strength – by infantry infiltration through avenues of weakness. Expansion of an advance in depth would be accelerated by constantly widening the *breadth* of penetration on the flanks while winning *depth* by leapfrogging ahead successive reserve formations and units. It was hoped that the enemy defences would crumble in confusion as a plethora of initial local penetrations coalesced into one wholesale rupture. The third factor in the Germans' favour was offered gratuitously by their opponents, whose preoccupation with attack over so many years had lost them the habit of defence. Suddenly the British had to reacquire the art at short notice and, in looking for a ready-made doctrine, adopted that devised by the Germans in 1917. But with only three months grace in which to build new type fortifications within

Bruchmüller's artillery: the old scene repeats itself

a scantily defined battle zone, they entered the same trap as had the Germans: they were to succumb to the temptation of giving way to pressure on the flanks when it was the overall planned intention to hold firm everywhere and await rescue by counter-attack. Thereby they actually encouraged German erosions by infiltration.

The dramatic early success of Operation 'Michael', as history relates, so shook the Allies as to make them repair their shattered illusions by a root and branch reorganisation of their command structure. General Foch became Generalissimo with powers exceeding those reached for unavailingly by Nivelle, the previous year. With this came political accord and unity of military direction just as the German armies were making for Amiens and threatening to separate the British from touch with the

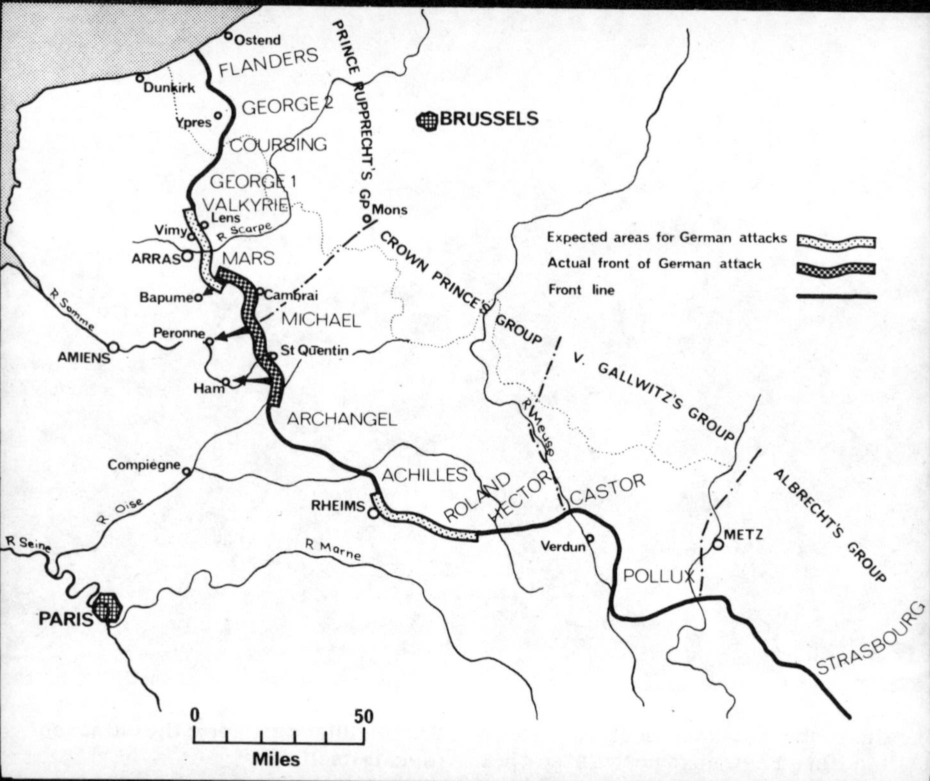

The area of the last major German offensive of the war

French army. Yet at this very moment, when a German victory of vast proportions seemed almost assured, they suffered setbacks near Arras where Ludendorff and Rupprecht most earnestly desired to make progress. Brusque rebuffs by the British Third Army under Byng led to a cloying constriction of expanding conquest and to recriminations within the German camp. Von Kuhl, Rupprecht's Chief of Staff, saw each multiplication of effort, to exploit every enemy weakness as it appeared, as leading to an over-stretching of the German army's offensive capacity. As a result Ludendorff, on the telephone to Rupprecht, became 'quite beside himself and dissatisfied' with Kuhl. Of 'Michael's' eight pre-planned successors, the first to be actuated – Operation 'Mars' – was intended to seize Arras and Vimy Ridge – but only on a contingency basis. Realising the strength in which the Canadians and British had entrenched the area Ludendorff withheld an assault until evidence of intending enemy withdrawal became available. It was not long coming for, although Haig retained a disproportionate part of his strength at the Arras hinge, it was in front of Arras, on 22nd March, that Byng felt compelled to economise in frontage and withdraw from Monchy le Preux to a shorter line closer to the city. This withdrawal, undetected by the Germans for several hours, acted as the green light for Ludendorff's sanction of 'Mars' and its execution for 28th March. He read only what he wanted to recognise and, in the euphoria of victory in the south, saw potential victory everywhere.

At this time there was also local dissention in the Allied camp. Currie, the Canadian Corps Commander, whose men had shared with most other British divisions the holocaust of Passchendaele in the Third Battle of Ypres, now resisted Haig's desire to fill gaps, caused by 'Michael', with individual Canadian Divisions taken piecemeal from his corps. Eventually the corps would be emptied and relegated to reserve. And this he could not stomach. Recognising that, as C-in-C, Haig would 'do as he thinks best', Currie nevertheless contended that Canadians would only fight well on their own as a corps, and he invoked political pressures to gain his point. In response Haig, all too aware of inherent mistrust of his policies by his Government at home while he conducted a desperate battle to save his army and the war, could reason that Currie was motivated more by nationalistic tendencies than feelings for the common good: 'He wishes only to fight as a Canadian Corps', wrote Haig. In the upshot some Canadian divisions were actually taken into army reserve, but the corps remained intact, eventually taking its turn holding an extended sector that stretched from Lens past Arras. But when Operation 'Mars' began on the 28th they merely held the Ridge and the Lorette Spur and thus were in an ideal position to judge for themselves how well six divisions of their British cousins were fighting when pitted against the fifteen committed by the Germans.

Rupprecht's concentration of artillery for 'Mars' effected an even greater density of guns per yard of front than had been assembled for 'Michael' at its strongest point. But the seven weeks granted to occupy the 'Michael' emplacements were now reduced to only nine days for the redeployment of facilities from the south. Indeed the Germans were to claim that time was too short to make adequate preparations. Yet relentlessly those preparations went ahead under strict discipline and control. A contemporary account catches the systematic precision of it all. 'The routes and battle positions of infantry and artillery are marked on the maps issued. Each battalion is allocated a guide from its division . . . There is precise marching order and no slowing down permitted . . . Absolute silence, no lights, no clatter of equipment, no clanking of wheels, no rattle of vehicles; wheels

The masses advance

to be bound with wood shavings and wire wool'. Nevertheless, practised as the Germans now were in secretly shifting and concealing thousands of guns and millions of shells in close proximity to a new front, so too were the British proficient in detecting their presence. So while German munitions and guns slipped skilfully by night into carefully pre-reconnoitred and marked emplacements, and did all in their power to hide the traces from prying aircraft, British Intelligence gathered innumerable reports of appearing flags such as were used to guide the gun teams into position, the ammunition trains and wagon columns trundling ceaselessly by night, and the fresh divisions crowding nearer the front. Thus when the all enveloping roar of guns thundered out at 0300 hours on the 28th the British were as near ready as they could be to withstand the shock, and their artillery replied with almost as good as it got when the German infantry stormed into the assault.

One thing 'Mars' lacked, from which 'Michael' had profited, was early morning mist to conceal the primary advance of the infantry. Although the German bombardment engulfed the British lines, setting the horizon ablaze with its twinkling explosions in the dark and mixing gas clouds with the haze of breaking dawn, visibility overall was so excellent that, from the high ground on either side of Arras, the battlefield spread clear like a diorama. In the ghostly stillness immediately preceding the bombardment, the German infantry were observed filing into the assault trenches, and soon the sky was traced by flares, those of the British calling down SOS tasks from their artillery, others from the Germans signalling success or demanding special artillery concentrations on unsubjugated defenders. South and north of the Scarpe, in a phased assault, the Germans broke among the forward British trenches infiltrating like ferrets in a burrow. A week before similar tactics to these had undone the defenders who, sensitive to flank pressure, gave way everywhere once even a local penetration had been made. Now it was different, as units better briefed tended to stand firm once by-passed and await rescue by counterattack.

North of the Scarpe the fighting was fiercest of all and the more dangerous for the threat it posed to the defenders of the Ridge – the key to the operation. Here I Bavarian Corps employed seven divisions where their bombardment had all but obliterated the front line trenches – trenches which, in accordance with the new system, were held in strength only at night and lightly by day. Quickly the leading skirmishers came to close quarters, an observer from 4th Division recording how, 'One man walked in a stooping position with a gun fastened to his back while others rotated and fired. I am sure this accounted for a large number of our casualties as the bullets were skimming the tops of our trenches'. On the front of 2nd Battalion Essex Regiment near Gavrelle the Germans burst suddenly among the defenders, '. . . the headquarters staff had only just time to escape, leaving a bonfire of papers and maps, for as they left one trench the enemy appeared at the other'. German aircraft dived across the trenches squirting machinegun fire at the crouching occupants. Frequently there were grenade to grenade exchanges between desperate men at a range of fifteen feet. A signaller recalled how, '. . . we scrambled over the mountains of debris – pieces of duckboard, wire, iron stakes and earth inextricably mixed up. Then we came across men of the battalion in support and it was here that a strong defence line existed . . . in all about thirty-five

The British retreat

Above: A check in the flow. *Below:* Assault artillery in the open; but they were outclassed on the approaches to Vimy Ridge

other ranks put into position on fire steps while others were posted on the sunken road which ran from the riverside village of Fampoux towards Gavrelle . . . Various items of information – and rumour – began to reach us. Jerry is coming down the road towards us from Gavrelle. Our companies have been practically wiped out'.

But rumour-mongers in war are usually the swiftest runners and in this instance almost wholly false. Nowhere did the Germans break through because the British guns, emplaced either on the forward slope in full view of the enemy, or with their observers on the crest and granted a clear sight of their targets, closed the front with fire. The attack broke down, lost its rhythm, cohesion and momentum. German infantry, who had advanced weighed heavily down with blankets, extra boots, several days rations and quantities of ammunition, in the misconception of pursuing a defeated opponent, fell dead and wounded as lumbering targets to British infantry and artillerymen who had a field day. British field guns fired the highest ever recorded number of rounds in a single day – 750 rounds each while the howitzers loosed off 650 each. Many guns, staying in action on the forward edge of the battle, were kept supplied with ammunition by wagons galloped up under fire – those same guns enjoying a distinct advantage over German assault gunners who were forced to drag their pieces into the front line with little chance of settling into position for accurate work. It would have been better had the Germans used tanks, for this was tanks' work, but they had less than a score of which none at all were at Arras and, in a gun versus gun duel, were everywhere worsted. So the German assault drew to its inevitable end, stopped well short of the crest at the Point du Jour, and even before dusk British patrols began to seek them out where they lay exhausted on territory so recently captured. Indeed, the British scented victory just when Ludendorff, Rupprecht and others recognised the significance of this rebuff. Not only had 'Mars' been killed stone dead but its defeat ensured the eventual demise of 'Michael' as it struggled with daily diminishing success to the south. The next intended Operation – 'Valkyrie', set for the following day and supplemental to 'Mars', to gain possession of of the Lorette Spur – had to be cancelled without option. Ludendorff had no other alternative but turn to secondary projects – the 'George' operations aimed against the Ypres Salient, which were to extract from Haig his celebrated 'backs to the wall' appeal and later still the attempts to reach Paris which were to end in as thorough a repulse by the French and Americans as was to be achieved on the British fronts.

Throughout these tense encounters the Canadian Corps acted as an onlooker; gradually to take over a greater share of the front opposite Arras while nurturing its strength for a task as yet undefined. The day was soon to come when they alone in the Allied camp would have the ability and rested strength to operate as a fresh entity in swinging the battle the Allied way once the German offensives had expended their impetus. By default they acquired the vitality of a power in being; carefully watched by the Germans in the reasoned belief that wherever the Canadians might appear, there a strong counter offensive could be expected. Thus the Arras front attracted ceaseless German vigilance from April to mid-July whenever the Canadian Corps took a turn in the line. And on 22nd July this was put to diversionary account by Currie's simulation of preparations for an attack south of the Scarpe in the direction of Monchy. But the Canadians' true destiny in 1918 was to be found further south yet, where, close by Amiens, the Allies were to begin the main offensive which was to bring the war to an end.

The final sally

July was the month when the Allies got the full measure of the German offensive, August the one in which they turned it to their own advantage. As each of Ludendorff's attempts to break through met with tougher resistance and progressively smaller gains, the recoil of British and French counterattacks became swifter and more lucrative. German soldiers began to lose their resilience in attack and their defiance in defence. They surrendered more easily when attacked with increased vigour. Although he refused to admit it, Ludendorff's throw for victory was spent by the end of July, even as he planned yet one more attempt against the British in Flanders. But General Foch had other ideas and on 24th July he was putting in motion the train of orders that were to be converted into a great Anglo-French attack with over 500 tanks at Amiens on 8th August.

For this attack the Canadian Corps was to be used complete along with the Australian Corps, British III and Cavalry Corps, and the First French Army. On the Allied side 3,676 guns of various calibres would support an attack on a twenty-mile front. Here, as at Cambrai and in all subsequent onslaughts, the guns were to withhold their fire until the moment of attack while the troops taking part would occupy their assault positions at the last possible moment and in the greatest possible secrecy. This the Allies could do so much better than the Germans because the tanks, which did the artillery's previous work of cutting the wire, needed only to arrive at the very last moment and required no prolonged and obvious dumping of ammunition to prepare their efforts or divulge their presence to German aircraft which, in any case, were hard pressed to seek them out because of the overwhelming Allied air superiority. Deception measures on the Allied side were legion. The Canadians, who secretly began their journey from Arras on 30th July, even set up radio stations in Flanders to give the impression that this was the destination of the entire Corps, and maintained their bogus signal traffic until 6th August.

The effect of the attack on 8th August was to do far more than break the German line, reap a vast haul of guns and prisoners, and push in a dent some seven miles deep on the first day. It was to crack German confidence in the future and to so undermine Ludendorff's resolve that he peremptorily called for diplomatic moves to end the war. We know that Ludendorff suffered

Last post in the Hindenburg Line

from a toxic goitre which could easily have been the cause of his nervous tension, alarmist tendencies and bouts of physical collapse. It is possible that had the crack in his confidence not been publicised the war might have lasted longer. But perhaps the Kaiser also leapt prematurely at a chance to end it all. The fact is that, within a few days, the German army began to put a brake on Allied progress and, though subsequent penetrations brought local débacles in their train and a large scale withdrawal towards the German frontier, there was evidence available that further prolonged resistance was feasible if the will to persevere had been maintained. But the headstrong pull for peace, permitted by a slackening of the reins of leadership, could not be reversed once allowed. From 8th August onward all successive Allied attacks brought substantial advances in their train, the ripples of progress eddying outwards, north and south of Amiens, until, within a fortnight, they lapped the ramparts of Arras once more.

Haig, as vastly encouraged as Ludendorff was depressed, looked keenly for an end to the war in 1918, as opposed to his political masters in London who saw it only as a possibility in 1919. On many previous occasions Haig had deluded himself into thinking the enemy was on his last legs: now he just happened to be right. But the problem of executing a series of pushes against successive sectors of the front was contingent upon the provision of fresh men, the swift redeployment of artillery and its ammunition, and the number of tanks available. The British infantry was tired, though fighting well under the spur of success; the artillery was more flexible and handy than ever; but the tanks were to be reduced by losses and breakdown from a strength of 1,184 on the 8th to 266 fit for action on 31st August. By 25th August they were already being rationed at the front.

Under these circumstances the freshest troops were bound to be used more intensively than others and so no sooner had the Canadians ceased operations in the vicinity of Amiens than they were being withdrawn and sent secretly north again, back to Arras where they were to carry out in reality the attack towards Monchy such as they had discussed as a blind in July. But whereas in July there had been a hectic argument between Currie and one of his divisional commanders concerning the magnitude of massed tank assault the ground warranted, by 26th August, when the real thing was to start, a mere eighteen could be provided and those tied down by a stipulation that they were not to lead the attack unless 'definite resistance' made their use imperative. It was a sign of the times, of course, that 'definite resistance' was not considered wholly likely.

The Germans on either side of the Scarpe indubitably invited attack for they had thinned out the line and held it now with little more than the equivalent of two divisions. They were to be attacked by the British 51st Division north of the river and the 3rd and 2nd Canadian Divisions to the south – the latter dovetailing their advance, just to the north of Neuville Vitasse, with the advance of XVII Corps where it bored up from the south on the tide of the Amiens success. First Army, still under Horne, was responsible for the Scarpe attack and saw it as a closing up to the Drocourt – Quéant Line against an enemy who was prone to withdraw at call. Currie set as his objective for the first day a line running west of Monchy – the same as Allenby had hoped to achieve in a day in April 1917. Currie might have been further encouraged had he known that, in German 39th Division opposing him, little encouragement was given to opposition since '. . . the commitment of the Canadians, the best British troops, had been recognised'. Ludendorff might insist upon his men holding out well forward of the Hindenburg Line in order to wear out the enemy before they reached

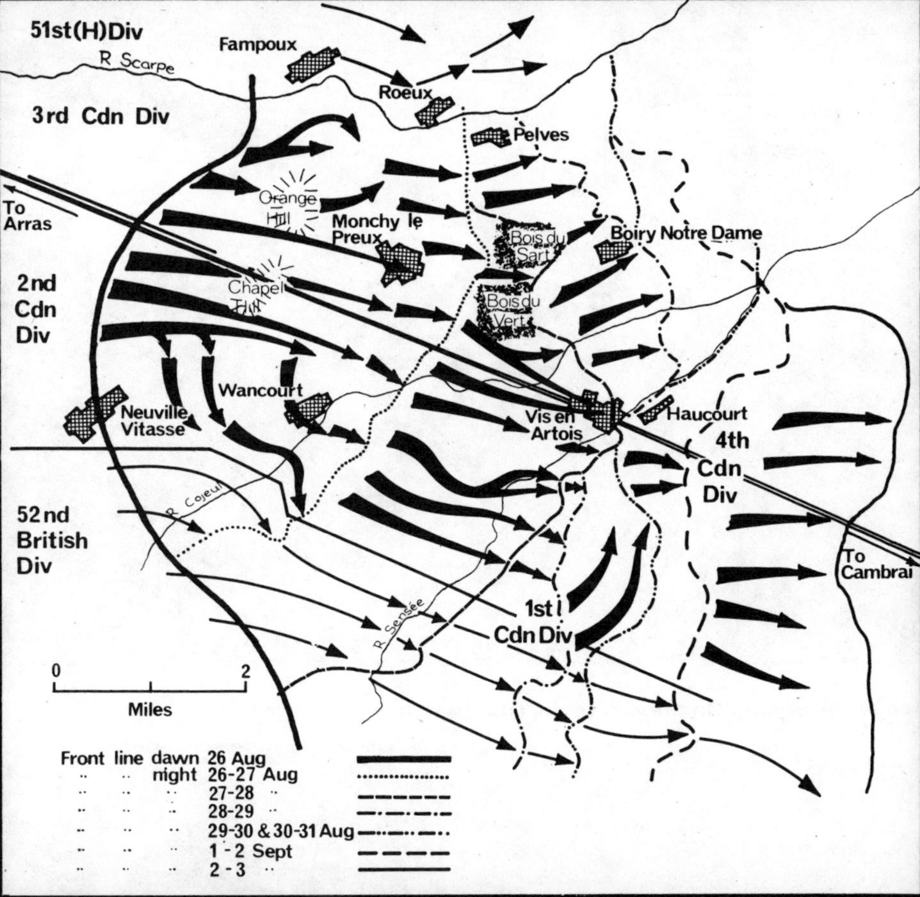

The Canadian role in the final British pushes, August to September 1918

Above and below: On the way to the DQ Switch

the strongest position, but his subordinates and men knew better and dealt otherwise.

Currie, whose attack was to go in shortly before dawn on the 26th, had worries of his own, however. The bare handful of tanks was delayed and did not arrive until two hours after dawn, when several developed mechanical faults. The bright moonlight of the previous nights was dimmed by cloud and rain, making direction keeping in the early stages of the attack an uncertain practice. But the support of fourteen field and nine heavy brigades of artillery caused a most comforting noise and proved adequate with its major commitment to counterbattery work on the German guns. Yet Currie need not have worried, for the wire, not nearly as thick as had once been the case, had been well cut by the guns and the German artillery was suppressed. North of the Scarpe his flank was kept secure by 51st Division advancing in step, clearing the approaches to Roeux with ease where, fifteen months earlier, this same division had suffered appalling losses for no permanent gain. Second Canadian Mounted Rifles made for Orange Hill; their story related by their Commanding Officer as they felt their way round the northern shoulder of the hill, out of sight of many German machinegunners:

'This morning at zero there was no fog; now and again the moon would break through the rain and clouds, giving a little light. The same old roar of guns and bursting shells, but this time we were tight up behind the barrage and the sight was wonderful. The flash of the shell bursts showed the men moving steadily forward with fixed bayonets, many of them smoking and joking. Our plans worked perfectly; as we moved up the flank of the hill we could see the flashes from the German machineguns firing to their front down the slope until stopped by the bombs or bayonets of our men taking them in flank. One sacrifice [anti-tank] 77mm field gun was also taken in this way, the gunners dying at their gun, which was afterwards swung round and used against its previous masters. By 5am the hill was ours and the 1st and 5th CMR passed through to Monchy.'

German resistance was only spasmodic and largely complementary to the Canadians' tactics, for while the latter aimed to exploit weakness the Germans presented little in the way of strength to bar their way. As was usual in infantry combat, the work of individuals played a key part. While tanks began to arrive one by one in the forefront of the advance and aircraft darted ahead to superimpose bombing and machinegunning from low level, aimed at German emplacements, upon the artillery fire, a Lieutenant Rutherford of 5th CMR won the Victoria Cross by capturing Monchy practically singlehanded with a series of grenade attacks on machinegun posts from which seventy prisoners were taken.

Phase by phase, the Canadians developed their attack, infiltrating the German lines, oozing round each island of resistance as its periphery was defined. And the Germans, knowing they were in no state to hold, fell back to the Bois du Sart Ridge to the east of Monchy whence they had started so hopefully, in March, prior to the ill-fated Operation 'Mars'. Reinforcements were taking up position and from here a coherent response could be made, first and foremost against tanks as, in solo defiance, they endeavoured to help the Canadian infantry. But in an open plain, with tank numbers so few, the German gunners knew little distraction from their primary task of tank destruction. Each slow moving hulk became the centre of a whirlpool of fire from numerous guns. No matter how inaccurate their zone of fire the guns were bound by the law of averages related to sheer output, to hit their target in the end. Then tank hulks, battered and broken, would become a feature of local tactical importance, fought over by opposing infantry patrols. The com-

mander of one crew, which had abandoned its vehicle to continue to fight on foot, heard the enemy had captured his machine for use as a pill-box, and so he returned and chased the enemy out of one sponson after entering by the opposite side.

As the day wore on the rain fell more heavily and German resistance magnified. Once more the valley between Monchy and Bois du Sart became the grave of Allied hopes, intense machine-gun fire sweeping the slopes and stopping all further progress. Tanks tried to get forward to loosen this opposition and simply fell victims in the valley alongside the pinned infantry. And here again the hulks were the centre of hand-to-hand fighting. This day, however, the German High Command began to react in closer sympathy with its lower formations. Though Ludendorff still rejected an immediate withdrawal into the safety of the Hindenburg Line, his Army Group and army commanders were ever more strongly in favour of this course. Some realised that all thought of future counterattacks was useless, since it seemed to them they were being forced on to the defensive for good. Their dilemma was redoubled, however, by consideration of how to abandon the forward area without also losing the vast quantities of material stacked within its confines. It had taken months to accumulate the dumps and would take weeks to extract them from the enemy's grasp. Talk of mobile warfare – expansive cut and thrust – was therefore conditioned by the state of mind and posture into which years of static combat and the artillery juggernaut had thrown the armies.

Yet as the British and Canadians began to ease forward, leaving behind the miniature townships they had built near the battle zone, they too began to lose power. Within a couple of days, for instance, the two leading Canadian divisions advancing on

Guns move on, the wounded come back

Above: Canada's infantry in open country at last. *Below:* The pillboxes are over-run and left behind. *Below right:* Tanks, the final arbiters of the victory, advance from Vimy Ridge through the Hindenburg Line

5784

either side of the Arras/Cambrai road and outflanking the Bois du Sart Ridge, were approaching the extremes of exhaustion and badly in need of their 1st and 4th Divisions to take up the running long before they reached the Drocourt Queant Switch. On their left the 51st Division was keeping pace, but the problems of dragging forward guns and supplies were increasing. Moreover, the advantage obtained by observation from the creats of the ridge lessened with each new tactical bound that was taken. For these reasons Ludendorff's policy of over-straining his enemy in front of the Drocourt Queant switch was justified to a certain extent.

Much bitter fighting was to come as summer turned into autumn and the Allied advance drew closer to Germany. In a great convulsion, the British and Canadians were to expel the Germans, with one mighty heave, out of the Drocourt Queant Switch and burst through to Cambrai and then Mons where, for the British Army in 1914, the fighting had begun and where, for the Canadians, it was to end.

In the course of the war Vimy Ridge had witnessed a unique decline in the art of war and its partial recovery. It had seen the early mobile encounters; deadlock in the trenches; the first attempts to break that deadlock at the expense of Frenchmen torn to pieces by German guns; and eventually the replacement of men by machines of destruction. In the final engagements its importance had been reduced because its defences had grown so strong that neither side would tackle them without positive evidence that the other was ready to concede. The price in material for shuffling advances had been immense, and the price in lives incalculable. For every body enclosed in a grave there were many permanently maimed or totally obliterated.

That narrow belt of land, little more than five miles deep, which reaches either side of Arras and Vimy Ridge

and extends to slightly greater depth in places where it stretches northward to the sea and south to the Swiss frontier, contains a unique concentration of burial grounds. On Vimy Ridge itself is territory presented by France to the people of Canada as a gift to mark that nation's special sacrifice and her first great military achievement. The rows of graves lie between Canadian pines, dominated by the twin pylons of the monument towering on the heights, looking

On the heights of success, Canada's monument at Vimy

back whence the assault came on 9th April 1917, and forwards across the Plain of Douai where it failed. Here the soil bears its own testimony to four years' struggle. One short stretch of trench has been preserved as part of the Canadian memorial. Across the remainder, old communication trenches intersect; great craters plunge where the mines blew up; and miles of tunnels burrow beneath the solid chalk and stretch far underground, their sides engraved with the initials of fighting men who passed that way to await the call to surface and face the enemy. Where undergrowth is rank and uncut the notice boards warn of a hidden peril – the unexploded shell, its charge volatile with age, its effect upon those who tamper with it as potentially disastrous as on the day it was fired.

Bibliography

Allenby, Soldier and Statesman by AP Wavell (Harrap, London)
British Official History of the War, Military Operations: France and Belgium 1917 (Macmillan, London)
The Canadian Expeditionary Force 1914-1919 by GWL Nicholson (Canadian Department of National Defense)
Der Weltkrieg 1914-1918 compiled by OKH (Mittler)
Die Osterschlacht bei Arras 1917 (Reichsarchiv)
Field-Marshal Sir Henry Wilson by CE Callwell (Cassell, London)
Gunners at War by S Bidwell (Arms and Armour Press, London)
My War Memories by Erich von Ludendorff (Hutchinson, London)
The Pathology of Leadership by Hugh L'Etang (Heinemann, London)